P9-DMY-382

DYNAMICS—THE GEOMETRY OF BEHAVIOR

PART 2: CHAOTIC BEHAVIOR

VISMATH: THE VISUAL MATHEMATICS LIBRARY

VOLUME 2

## THE VISUAL MATHEMATICS LIBRARY
Ralph H. Abraham, Editor

*VISMATH BOOKS:*

VOLUME 0: Abraham and Shaw, MANIFOLDS AND MAPPINGS

VOLUME 1: Abraham and Shaw, DYNAMICS—THE GEOMETRY OF BEHAVIOR
      Part 1: Periodic Behavior

VOLUME 2: Abraham and Shaw, DYNAMICS—THE GEOMETRY OF BEHAVIOR
      Part 2, Chaotic Behavior

VOLUME 3: Abraham and Shaw, DYNAMICS— THE GEOMETRY OF BEHAVIOR
      Part 3: Global Behavior

VOLUME 4: Abraham & Shaw, DYNAMICS— THE GEOMETRY OF BEHAVIOR
      Part 4: Bifurcation Behavior

*VISMATH COMPUTER GRAPHIC PROGRAMS:*

DISK 1: Abraham  and Norskog, PHASE PORTRAITS IN THE PLANE

DISK 2: Abraham and Norskog, CHAOTIC ATTRACTORS IN 3D

DISK 3: Abraham and Norskog, BIFURCATION EXPERIMENTS

*VISMATH LIBRARY FILM SERIES*

THE LORENZ SYSTEM: Bruce Stewart, 25 minutes, color 16mm.

CHAOTIC CHEMISTRY: Robert Shaw, Jean-Claude Roux and Harry Swinney, 20 minutes,
      black & white, 16 mm.

CHAOTIC ATTRACTORS OF DRIVEN OSCILLATORS : J. P. Crutchfield, 12 minutes,
      black & white, 16 mm.

## THE SCIENCE FRONTIER EXPRESS SERIES

THE DRIPPING FAUCET AS A MODEL CHAOTIC SYSTEM, Robert Shaw
ON MORPHODYNAMICS, Selected papers by Ralph Abraham
COMPLEX DYNAMICAL SYSTEMS, Selected papers by Ralph Abraham

## Series Foreword

During the Renaissance, algebra was resumed from Near Eastern sources, and geometry from the Greek. Scholars of the time became familiar with classical mathematics. When calculus was born in 1665, the new ideas spread quickly through the intellectual circles of Europe. Our history shows the importance of the diffusion of these mathematical ideas, and their effects upon the subsequent development of the sciences and technology.

Today, there is a cultural resistance to mathematical ideas. Due to the widespread impression that mathematics is difficult to understand, or to a structural flaw in our educational system, or perhaps to other mechanisms, mathematics has become an esoteric subject. Intellectuals of all sorts now carry on their discourse in nearly total ignorance of mathematical ideas. We cannot help thinking that this is a critical situation, as we hold the view that mathematical ideas are essential for the future evolution of our society.

The absence of visual representations in the curriculum may be part of the problem, contributing to mathematical illiteracy, and to the math-avoidance reflex. This series is based on the idea that mathematical concepts may be communicated easily in a format which combines visual, verbal, and symbolic representations in tight coordination. It aims to attack math ignorance with an abundance of visual representations.

In sum, the purpose of this series is to encourage the diffusion of mathematical ideas, by presenting them *visually*.

THE VISUAL MATHEMATICS LIBRARY: VISMATH VOLUME 2

# DYNAMICS—THE GEOMETRY OF BEHAVIOR

Part 2: Chaotic Behavior

With 170 illustrations

by

Ralph H. Abraham

and

Christopher D. Shaw

University of California
Santa Cruz, CA 95064

Aerial Press, Inc.
P.O.Box 1360, Santa Cruz, California, 95061

Library of Congress Cataloging in Publication Data

Library of Congress Catalog Card Number: 81-71616

ISBN 0-942344-02-2 (Volume 2)
ISBN 0-942344-00-6 (4 volume set)


Second Printing: March, 1984
Third Printing: March, 1985

Original text reproduced by Aerial Press, Inc., from camera-ready copy prepared by the authors. Copyright © by Aerial Press, Inc,

Printed in the United States of America.

CONTENTS

Preface                                                                    ix
Historical Introduction                                                     1

Ch. 1. STATIC LIMIT SETS AND CHARACTERISTIC EXPONENTS                        5

    1.1 Limit points in one dimension                                       7
    1.2 Saddle points in two dimensions                                    13
    1.3 Nodal points in two dimensions                                     17
    1.4 Spiral points in two dimensions                                    21
    1.5 Critical points in three dimensions                                27

Ch. 2. PERIODIC LIMIT SETS AND CHARACTERISTIC MULTIPLIERS                   31

    2.1 Limit cycles in the plane                                          33
    2.2 Limit cycles in a Möbius band                                      39
    2.3 Saddle cycles in three dimensions                                  43
    2.4 Nodal cycles in three dimensions                                   49
    2.5 Spiral cycles in three dimensions                                  53
    2.6 Characteristic exponents                                          59
    2.7 Discrete power spectra                                             63

Ch. 3. CHAOTIC LIMIT SETS                                                   67

    3.1 Poincare's solenoid                                                69
    3.2 Birkhoff's bagel                                                   77
    3.3 Lorenz's mask                                                      85
    3.4 Rössler's band                                                     89

Ch. 4. ATTRIBUTES OF CHAOS                                                  97

    4.1 Unpredictability                                                   99
    4.2 Divergence and information gain                                   107
    4.3 Expansion, compression, and charateristic exponents              113
    4.4 Fractal microstructure                                           121
    4.5 Noisy power spectra                                               127

CONCLUSION                                                                 133

APPENDIX: Systems of equations                                            135

BIBLIOGRAPHY                                                               137

INDEX                                                                     139

# Preface to the Dynamics Books

### what is dynamics?

Dynamics is a field emerging somewhere between mathematics and the sciences. In our view, it is the most exciting event on the concept horizon for many years. The new concepts appearing in dynamics extend the conceptual power of our civilization, and provide new understanding in many fields.

### the visual math format

We discovered, while working together on the illustrations for a book in 1978, that we could explain mathematical ideas visually, within an easy and pleasant working partnership. In 1980, we wrote an expository article on dynamics and bifurcations using hand-animation to emulate the *dynamic picture technique* universally used by mathematicians in talking among themselves: a picture is drawn slowly, line-by-line, along with a spoken narrative — the dynamic picture and the narrative tightly coordinated.

Our efforts inevitably exploded into four volumes of this series, of which this is the second. The dynamic picture technique, evolved through our work together, and in five years of computer graphic experience with the *Visual Math Project* at the University of California at Santa Cruz, is the basis of this work. About two-thirds of the books are devoted to visual representations, in which colors are used according to a strict code.

Moving versions of the phase portraits, *actual dynamic pictures,* will be made available as *computer graphic programs* on floppy disks for home computers, and as *videotapes, videodiscs, or films.*

### on the suppression of symbols

Math symbols have been kept to a minimum. In fact, they are almost completely suppressed. Our purpose is to make the book work for readers who are not practiced in symbolic representations. We rely exclusively on visual representations, with brief verbal explanations. Some formulas are shown with the applications, as part of the graphics, but are not essential. However, *this strategy is exclusively pedagogic.* We do not want anyone to think that we consider symbolic representations unimportant in mathematics. On the contrary, this field evolved primarily in the symbolic realm throughout the classical period. Even now, a full understanding of our subject demands a full measure of formulas, logical expressions, and technical intricacies from all branches of mathematics. Brief introductions to these are included as appendices in *Part One, Periodic Behavior.* The equations relevant for the chaotic systems described in this volume are included as an appendix at the end of this book.

## our goals

We have created these books as a short-cut to the research frontier of dynamical systems: theory, experiments, and applications. It is our goal — we know we may fail to reach it — to provide any interested person with an acquaintance with the basic concepts:

*state spaces: manifolds — geometric models for the virtual states of a system
*attractors: static, periodic, and chaotic — geometric models for the local asymptotic behavior of a system
*separatrices: repellors, saddles, insets, tangles — defining the boundaries of regions (basins) dominated by different behaviors (attractors), and characterizing the global behavior of a system.
*bifurcations: subtle and catastrophic — geometric models for the controlled change of one system into another.

The ideas included are selected from the literature of dynamics: *Part 1, Periodic Behavior,* covers the classical period from 1600 to 1950. (These are needed for all the following volumes.) This volume, *Part 2, Chaotic Behavior,* is devoted to recent developments, 1950 to the present, on the chaotic behavior observed in experiments. The sequels will be devoted to the theoretical developments, since 1950, belonging to the tradition begun by Poincaré.

## prerequisite background

We assume nothing in the way of prior mathematical training, beyond vectors in three dimensions, and complex numbers. Nevertheless, it will be tough going without a basic understanding of the simplest concepts of calculus. All the essential ideas will be presented in Volume 0 of this series.

## acknowledgements

Our first attempt at the pictorial style used here evolved in the first draft of *Dynamics, a Visual Introduction,* during the Summer of 1980. Our next effort, the preliminary draft of Volume 2 of this series, was circulated among friends in the Summer of 1981. Extensive feedback from them has been very influential in the evolution of this volume, and the whole series, and we are grateful to them:

Fred Abraham                     Jean-Pierre Eckman
Ethan Akin                          Len Fellman
Michael Arbib                       George Francis
Jim Crutchfield                    Alan Garfinkel
Larry Cuba                          John Guckenheimer
Richard Cushman                Moe Hirsch
Larry Domash                      Phil Holmes

Dan Joseph                 Katie Scott
Jean-Michel Kantor         Rob Shaw
Bob Lansdon                Mike Shub
Arnold Mandell             Steve Smale
Jerry Marsden              Joel Smoller
Jim McGill                 Jim Swift
Kent Morrison              Bob Williams
Charles Muses              Art Winfree
Norman Packard             Marianne Wolpert
Tim Poston                 Gene Yates
Otto Rössler               Chris Zeeman
Lee Rudolph

We are especially grateful to Tim Poston for his careful reading and extensive comments on the manuscript for this volume, to the Dynamics Guild (J. Crutchfield, D. Farmer, N. Packard, and R. Shaw) for their computer plots used in many places in this book, to Richard Cushman for history lessons, and to Claire Moore of Aerial Press for production guidance. The generosity and goodwill of many dynamicists has been crucial in the preparation of this book; we thank them all.

Ralph H. Abraham        Christopher D. Shaw

Santa Cruz, California        April, 1983

dedicated to
Henri Poincaré and George D. Birkhoff

# DYNAMICS
# THE GEOMETRY OF BEHAVIOR

## Part Two: Chaotic Behavior

# Historical Introduction

As described in Part One, experiments play an increasingly important role in dynamics. Helmholtz, Rayleigh, Duffing, Van der Pol, and Hayashi relied on experimental simulations to discover the main properties of periodic motions in nonlinear oscillations. Since 1950, digital simulations have become increasingly important, especially since the experimental discovery of chaotic attractors in 1962 by Lorenz.

But chaotic limit sets had been known to theoretical dynamics since Poincaré. The first chaotic attractor in a dynamical system (in the mathematical sense of a vector field on a state space) was discovered in 1932 by Birkhoff. It took many years before these objects emerged into the theoretical literature, in the works of Charpentier, Levinson, Cartwright, Littlewood, Smale, and others. Experimental studies accelerated this process.

But we must emphasize at once, and we cannot possibly do this as strongly as we would like, that *the connection between the chaotic attractors of theory, and those of experiments, is hypothetical at this time.*

In fact, many believe that the connection is fictitious. An account of this view may be found in the literature (Abraham, 1983a). But in this book, we will be very casual about this fundamental problem. We will speak of *chaotic attractor* in either the theoretical or experimental context.

This introduction presents a few words of description for some of the leading figures in the history of chaotic dynamics. Their positions in a two-dimensional tableau — date versus specialty (applied, mathematical, or experimental dynamics) — are shown in Table 1.

| Date | THEORY | EXPERIMENT |
|------|--------|------------|
| **TABLE 1.** **THE HISTORY OF CHAOTIC DYNAMICS** | | |
| 1850 | | |
| | Helmholtz | |
| | Poincaré | Rayleigh |
| 1900 | | |
| | | Duffing |
| | Birkhoff | Van der Pol |
| | Charpentier | |
| | Levinson | Hayashi |
| 1950 | Cartwright & Littlewood | |
| | | Lorenz, Stein & Ulam |
| | Smale | Rössler, Ueda |
| | | Shaw |
| 2000 | | |

**Here are some capsule histories. Further details may be found in Chapter 3.**

**Jules Henri Poincaré**, 1854-1912. In his studies of celestial motion, Poincaré discovered *homoclinic trajectories* (see Section 3.1). Eventually, in 1962, Smale showed that these are chaotic (non-attractive) limit sets. Thus the first appearance of a chaotic limit set in the mathematical literature, as far as we know, was in Poincaré's three volume work on celestial mechanics, in 1892.

**George David Birkhoff, 1884-1944.** The first chaotic attractor to appear in the mathematical literature, to our knowledge, is in Birkhoff's paper on remarkable curves, published in 1932. (See Section 3.2.) The actual discovery, in a context derived from celestial mechanics, occurred in 1916.

**Marie Charpentier.** Charpentier further developed the properties of Birkhoff's remarkable curves, in a series of papers in the 1930's.

**Norman Levinson.** In 1944, Levinson conjectured that Birkhoff's chaotic attractor might occur in the three-dimensional dynamics of forced oscillation. In 1948, he announced he had proved that it does.

**Mary Lucy Cartwright and J. E. Littlewood.** In a joint paper published in 1945, Cartwright and Littlewood announced a similar result. Their proof appeared in 1949. They were inspired by experimental observations of Van der Pol and Van der Mark, published in 1927.

**Edward N. Lorenz.** In one of the first digital simulations of a dynamical system, around 1961, Lorenz discovered the experimental object which has come to be known as a chaotic attractor, in the experimental sense. The took place in a model for atmospheric air currents.

**Stephen Smale.** In 1962, Smale proved that Poincaré's homoclinic trajectories are chaotic limit sets, in the mathematical sense.

More recently, there has been an enormous explosion of research work on both mathematical and experimental chaos. Reluctantly, we close our history at this point, in 1962.

# 1. Static Limit Sets and Characteristic Exponents

In *Part One, Periodic Behavior,* limit points and cycles in dimensions one, two, and three were introduced. In this chapter and the next, we review the geometry of these simple limit sets. Further, we introduce the *Liapounov characteristic exponents,* which completely characterize the geometry of the simple limit sets. This is prosaic, but important. In the third chapter, more complicated limit sets will be introduced.

## 1.1.   LIMIT POINTS IN ONE DIMENSION

In one-dimensional state spaces, dynamical systems are naturally very constrained. For example, the typical limit set must be a point. As in Part One, we begin with this case for completeness. In addition, this provides a simple context in which to describe a new idea, the *Liapounov characteristic exponent.*

**Recall that one-parameter state spaces were used extensively in the early history of science.**

**For example, George's temperature may be represented as a point on a line. A simple dynamical model for this experimental domain (George's oral temperature) could be the vector field shown here. It has a single point attractor. Starting with the thermometer at an arbitrary initial state (room temperature, say), he inserts it under his tongue. In three minutes, the transient dies away, leading to a static attractor.**

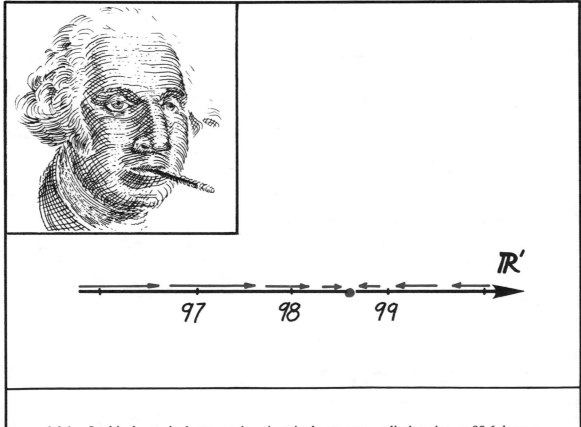

**1.1.1.**   In this dynamical system, there is a single attractor, a limit point, at 98.6 degrees.

We now describe the *characteristic exponent, or CE* of this limit point. Rotate each vector 90 degrees counterclockwise. Their ends delineate the *graph* of the vectorfield. In this context (one-dimensional linear state space) the graph is a curve in the two-dimensional plane. The graph goes through the horizontal axis at the limit point.

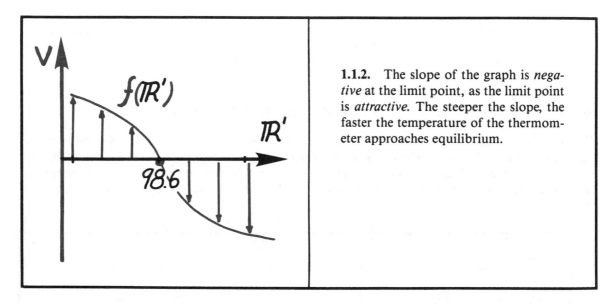

**1.1.2.** The slope of the graph is *negative* at the limit point, as the limit point is *attractive*. The steeper the slope, the faster the temperature of the thermometer approaches equilibrium.

There is only *one CE* because the dimension of the state space is *one*. In general, *the number of CEs is equal to the dimension of the state space.* Here, the dimension of the inset is one, which is maximal. The inset is an open subset of the state space. It is the *basin* of the point attractor. Meanwhile, the *outset* consists of a single point, the attractor. Thus, the *index* (dimension of the outset) is zero. The *magnitude of the CE* tells the *strength of the attractor,* that is, the rate of approach of the nearby trajectories, within the inset, or basin.

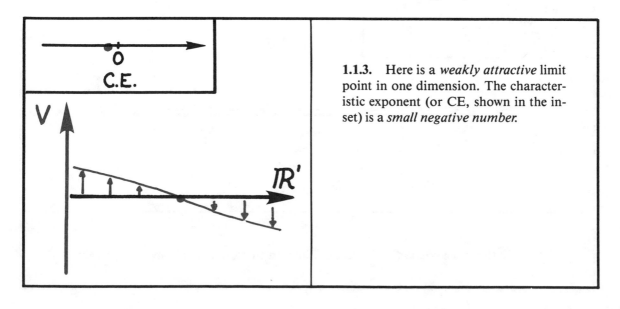

**1.1.3.** Here is a *weakly attractive* limit point in one dimension. The characteristic exponent (or CE, shown in the inset) is a *small negative number.*

**1.1.4.** The time series of typical trajectories (see *Part One)* in this system show a *gradual approach to the weakly attracting point.*

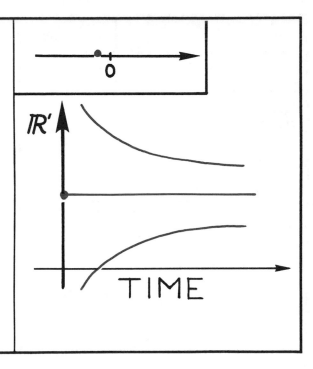

**1.1.5.** Here, in contrast, is a *strongly attracting* limit point. The characteristic exponent (see inset) is a *large negative number.*

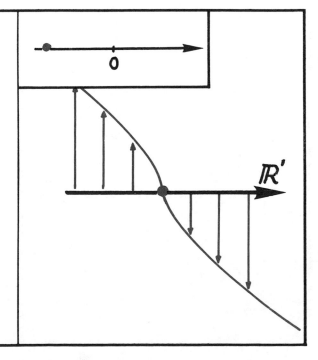

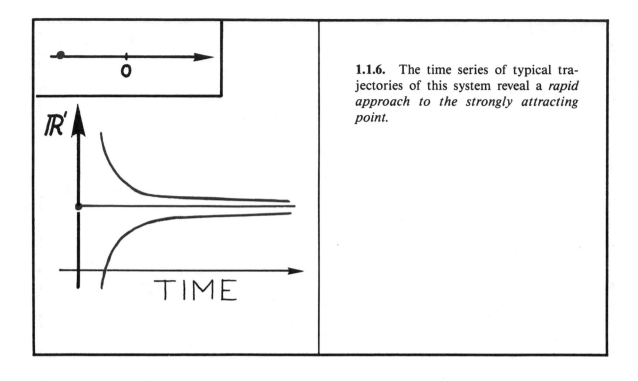

**1.1.6.** The time series of typical trajectories of this system reveal a *rapid approach to the strongly attracting point.*

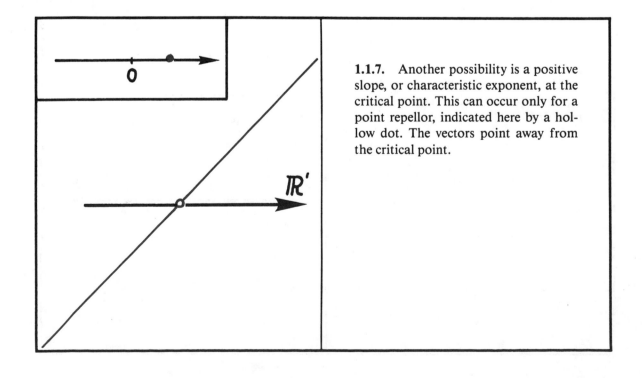

**1.1.7.** Another possibility is a positive slope, or characteristic exponent, at the critical point. This can occur only for a point repellor, indicated here by a hollow dot. The vectors point away from the critical point.

A limit point in one dimension is called *hyperbolic* if its CE is *not zero*. Some hyperbolic critical points in one dimension are shown in the following table.

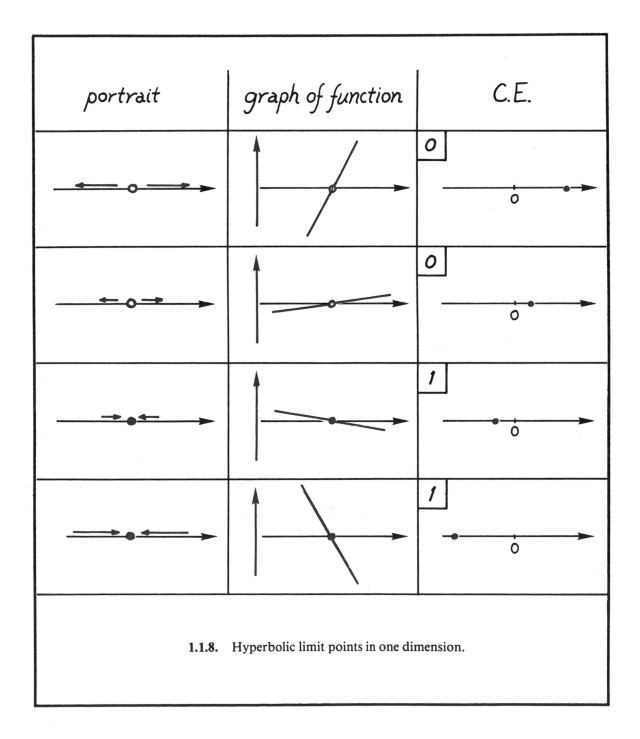

**1.1.8.**  Hyperbolic limit points in one dimension.

**What about zero as a CE? Zero slope implies tangency.**

A limit point with zero as its CE is called *nonhyperbolic* or *degenerate*.

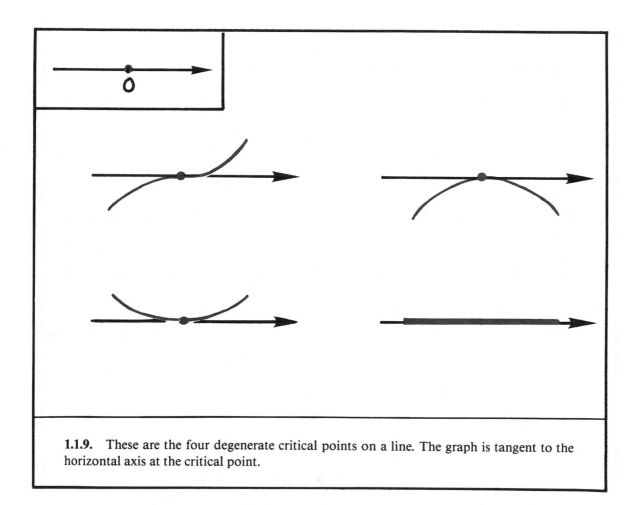

**1.1.9.** These are the four degenerate critical points on a line. The graph is tangent to the horizontal axis at the critical point.

In *Part Three* of this Series, we will explain how these degenerate cases are *exceptional*. Garden-variety dynamical systems do not have them. But they become important in the theory of *bifurcations,* treated in *Part Four* of this Series.

## 1.2.   SADDLE POINTS IN TWO DIMENSIONS

In *Part One,* we described limit points in the plane as nodal or spiral. Here we will characterize them in terms of their CEs.

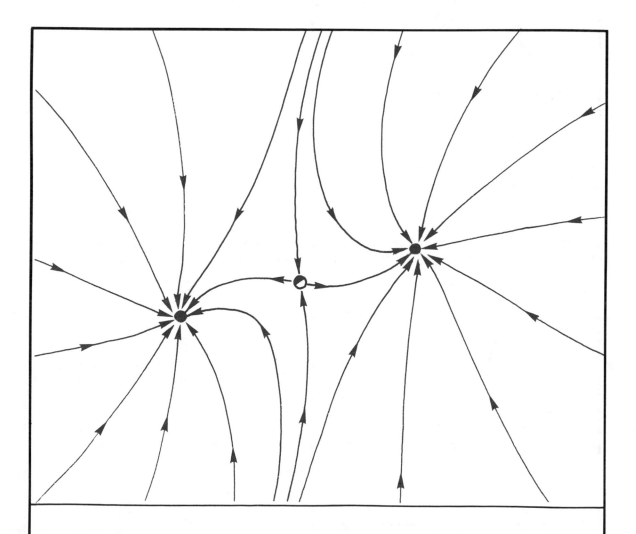

**1.2.1.**   Remember the phase portrait of the gradient system in *Part One* (1.6.10)? It has three limit points: two point attractors and a saddle point.

**Let's start with the saddle point. What are its CEs?**

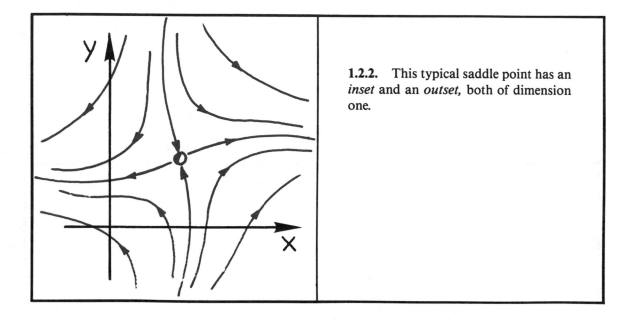

**1.2.2.** This typical saddle point has an *inset* and an *outset,* both of dimension one.

The *index* of this saddle is one.

To identify the two CEs of this saddle point, let's introduce a new coordinate system, by translation and rotation, so that the new coordinates start at the saddle, and are oriented along its inset and outset.

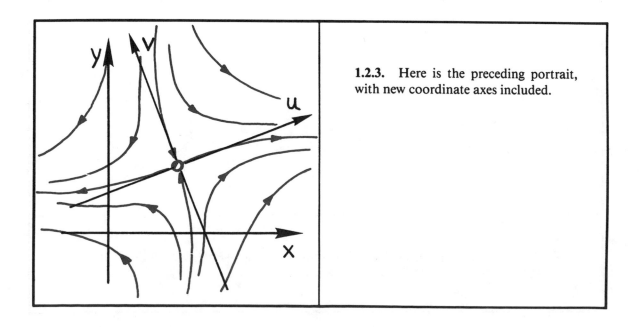

**1.2.3.** Here is the preceding portrait, with new coordinate axes included.

**1.2.4.** Here is the same portrait, rotated and translated, with the new coordinate axes in standard position.

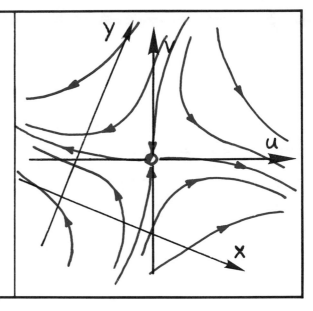

Now we suppose that we may treat each of the new coordinates separately. This seems to be assuming a lot, but it is actually justifiable.

**1.2.5.** Graphing the horizontal (u) component of the vector field (in the new coordinates) along the horizontal (u) axis, as in the preceding section, we may measure the slope, or *strength of repulsion,* in this direction. *This positive slope is one of the CEs of the saddle point.*

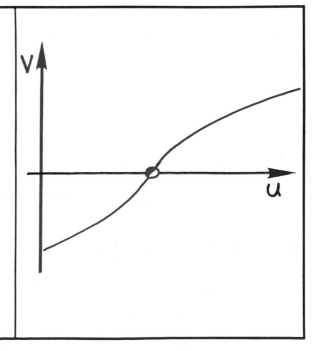

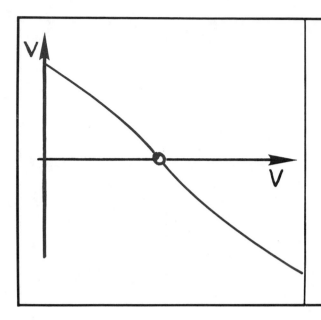

**1.2.6.** Likewise, graphing the vertical (v) component of the vectorfield, along the vertical (v) axis, we may measure the slope, or *strength of attraction,* in this direction. *This negative slope is the other CE of the saddle point.*

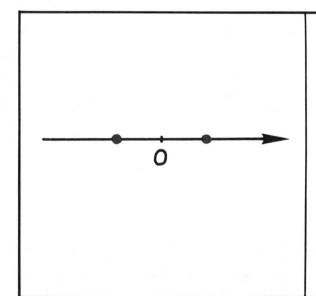

**1.2.7.** Here are the two CEs of the saddle point, pictured on the line of real numbers. One is negative, the other positive. As in the one-dimensional case, the CE to the left of the origin characterizes attraction, the one to the right, repulsion.

**Recall that the *index* of a critical point is the dimension of its outset. In this case, *the index is one*. And this is also the number of CEs to the right of zero.**

## 1.3.  NODAL POINTS IN TWO DIMENSIONS

Next we consider attractive critical points for dynamical systems in two dimensions. There are two types, nodal and spiral, as described in *Part One*. In this Section, we look at the nodal case. What are the CEs is this context? Let's consider a typical nodal attractor, as in the gradient system, 1.2.1.

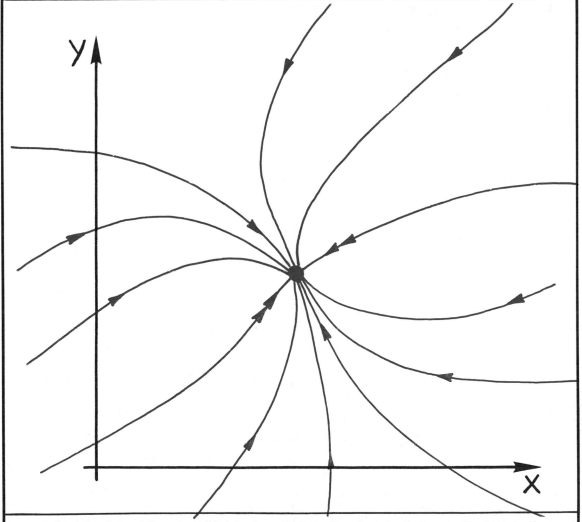

**1.3.1.**  Like the saddle point, this has characteristic directions (red). In one direction indicated by double arrows the attraction is stronger than in the other. We call this the *fast direction,* the other is the *slow direction.* The identification of these directions, for a nodal point, is not as easy as in the preceding case of a saddle point. Algorithms of linear algebra are normally used.

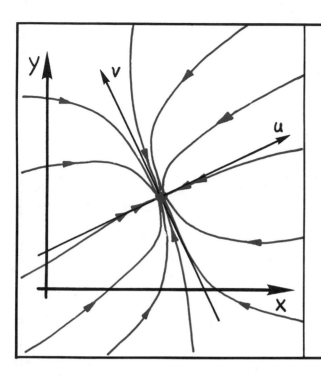

**1.3.2.** As with the saddle point, we introduce new coordinates centered at the attractive node, and oriented along the fast and slow directions.

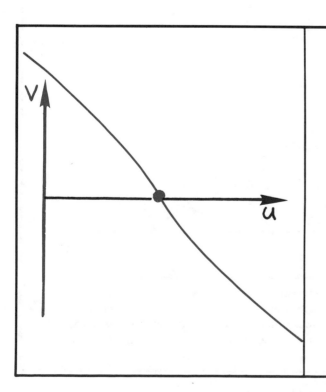

**1.3.3.** Graphing the component of the vectorfield along the new coordinate axis in the fast direction (u), we measure the slope of the graph at the critical point to obtain the fast CE. It is large and negative, characterizing fast (strong) attraction.

**1.3.4.** Graphing the component of the vectorfield along the slow (v) axis, the slope at the origin provides the slow CE. It is small and negative, characterizing slow (weak) attraction.

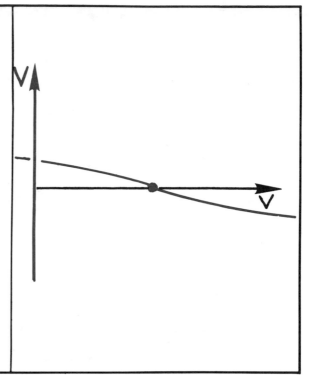

**1.3.5.** The two CEs are shown inset. The one to the left characterizes the stronger attraction of the fast direction. Both are to the left of zero, as the node is an attractor. To the right of zero there are no CEs, and the index of the nodal attractor is zero.

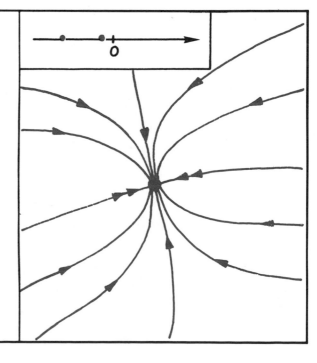

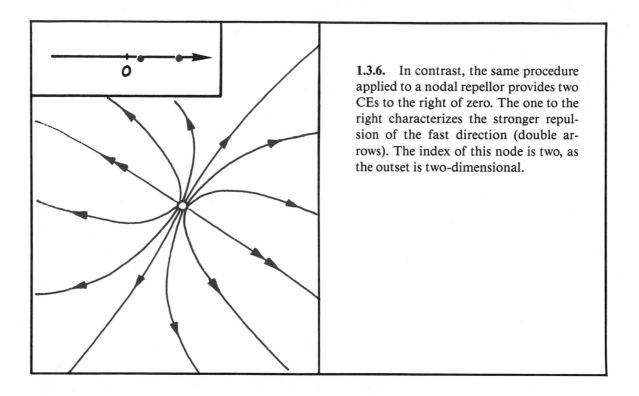

**1.3.6.**  In contrast, the same procedure applied to a nodal repellor provides two CEs to the right of zero. The one to the right characterizes the stronger repulsion of the fast direction (double arrows). The index of this node is two, as the outset is two-dimensional.

**In all hyperbolic cases, the index is equal to the number of CEs to the right of zero. This is zero for attractors, one for saddles, and two for repellors.**

## 1.4.   SPIRAL POINTS IN TWO DIMENSIONS

In two dimensions, there are two types of limit points, nodes and spirals. The spiral differs from a node in that there are no characteristic (fast and slow) directions.

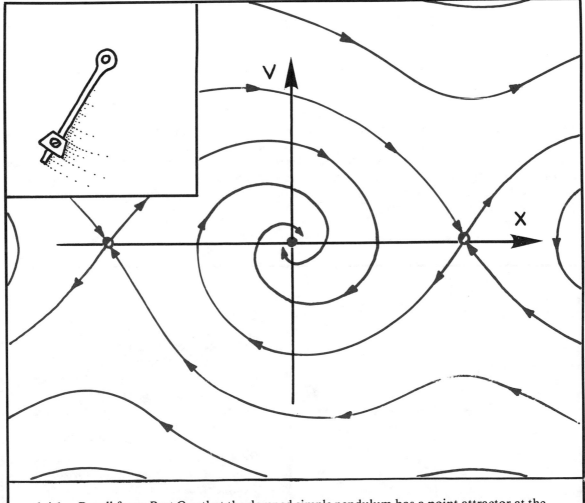

**1.4.1.**   Recall from *Part One* that the damped simple pendulum has a point attractor at the bottom, corresponding to an oscillation which dies away.

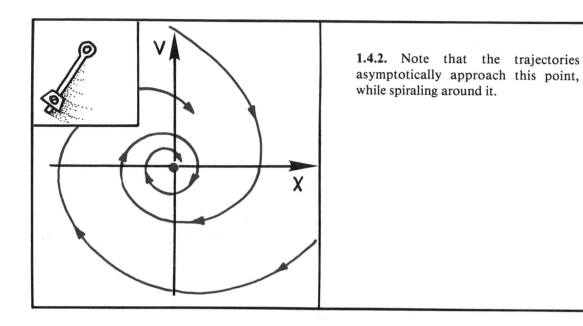

**1.4.2.** Note that the trajectories asymptotically approach this point, while spiraling around it.

The point attractor of spiral type, in the plane, also has two CEs. But they are not real numbers, and cannot be explained by reducing to the one-dimensional case. Instead, the vector field must be approximated, near the critical point, by a linear vectorfield. Linear algebra, applied to this approximation, provides two eigenvalues. These conjugate complex numbers are the CEs in this case. (For details, see Volume 0 of this Series.) This is also the actual procedure, using linear algebra, needed to calculate the CEs in the nodal case of the preceding section.

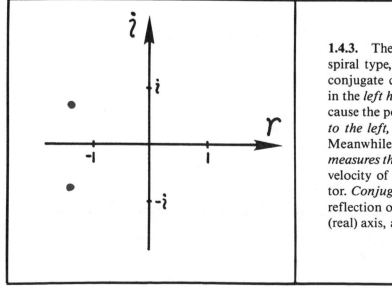

**1.4.3.** The CEs of a point attractor of spiral type, in the plane, are a pair of conjugate complex numbers. They are in the *left half* of the complex plane because the point is attracting: *the farther to the left, the stronger the attraction.* Meanwhile, their *vertical separation measures the rate of rotation,* or angular velocity of spiraling around the attractor. *Conjugate* means each is the mirror reflection of the other in the horizontal (real) axis, as shown here.

The set of CEs, pictured in the complex plane, is called the *spectrum* of the critical point.

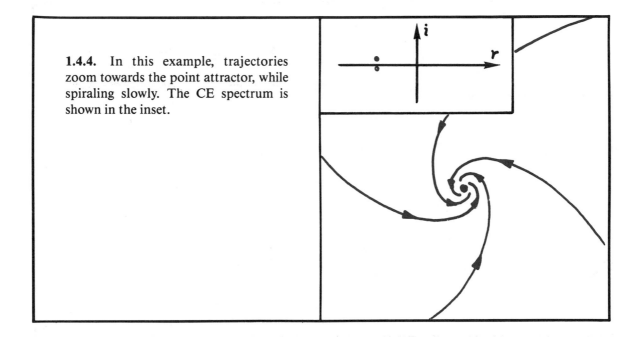

**1.4.4.** In this example, trajectories zoom towards the point attractor, while spiraling slowly. The CE spectrum is shown in the inset.

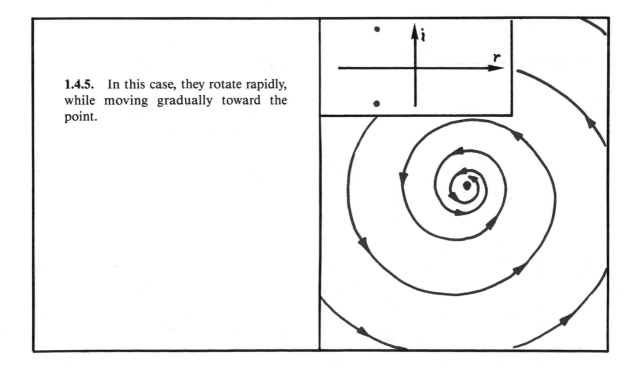

**1.4.5.** In this case, they rotate rapidly, while moving gradually toward the point.

**Remember: all attractors have index zero.**

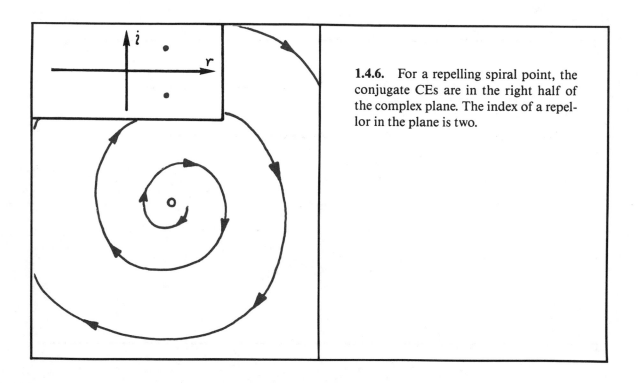

**1.4.6.** For a repelling spiral point, the conjugate CEs are in the right half of the complex plane. The index of a repellor in the plane is two.

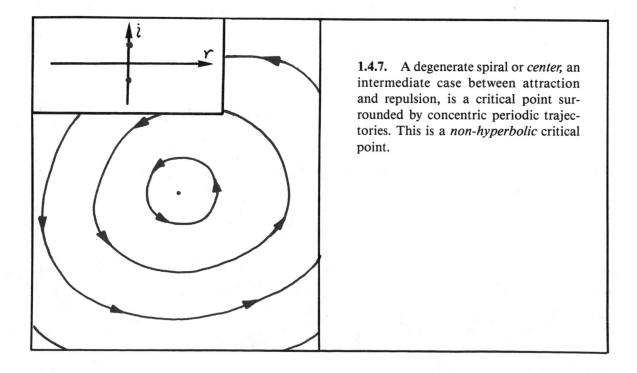

**1.4.7.** A degenerate spiral or *center,* an intermediate case between attraction and repulsion, is a critical point surrounded by concentric periodic trajectories. This is a *non-hyperbolic* critical point.

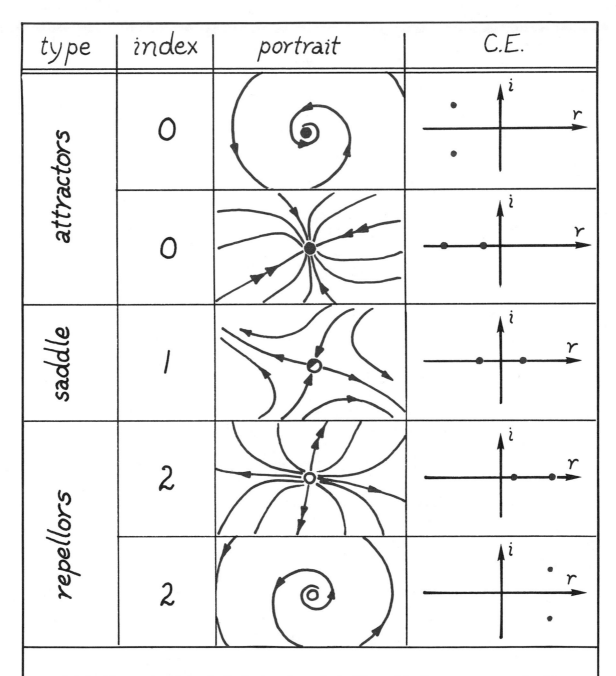

**1.4.8** The typical hyperbolic limit points, their CEs, and indices, are summarized in this table.

Actually, two cases are omitted from the table. These are the hyperbolic attractor and repellor with equal (real) CEs. They are classed among the degenerate cases, even though they are hyperbolic, because they are transitional phenomena between the nodal and spiral types. The cases shown are all the *elementary* ones, meaning hyperbolic, with distinct CEs.

### 1.5.    CRITICAL POINTS IN THREE DIMENSIONS

As in lower dimensions, critical points in three dimensions are mostly hyperbolic, with nonhyperbolic (degenerate) cases occurring exceptionally. We begin with the typical cases, which are hyperbolic. These may all be constructed by combining the hyperbolic linear and planar critical points of the preceding sections, in a single, three-dimensional portrait.

**We begin with a three-dimensional saddle point. There are three CEs for a critical point in three dimensions.**

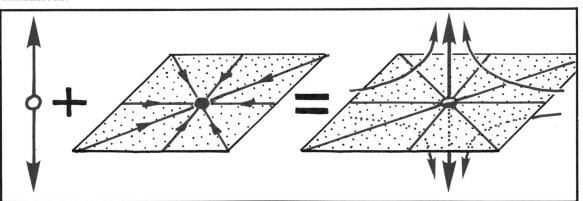

**1.5.1.** Here, a one-dimensional repellor is combined with a nodal attractor in a plane, to form a nodal saddle in three dimensions. In this case the linear component comprises the outset, which is one-dimensional. The planar component comprises the inset, which is two-dimensional. The sum of these dimensions is three, the total dimension of the state space, and the index is one. The trajectories which are neither in the inset nor in the outset fly by hyperbolically.

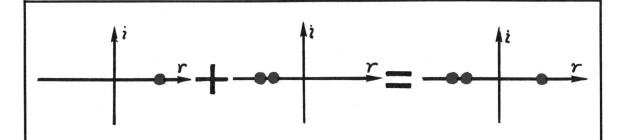

**1.5.2.**    There are three CEs for a critical point in three dimensions. Here are all three, for the nodal saddle point, pictured in the complex plane. All are real numbers in this case. The two in the left half-plane are the CEs of the attractive planar node, comprising the inset. The other is the CE of the linear repellor. Thus, the CEs for the combined critical point are just the CEs of the components.

**This is another example of this construction.**

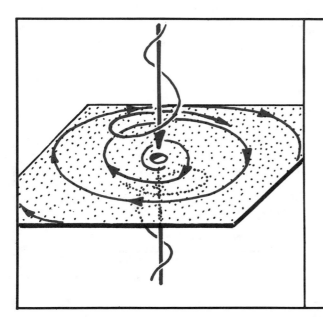

**1.5.3.** Here a planar repellor of spiral type is combined with a linear attractor, to form a spiraling saddle point in three dimensions. This time, the planar component comprises the outset, which is two-dimensional, so the index is two. The linear component comprises the inset. Trajectories neither in the outset nor the inset fly by, spiraling as they go.

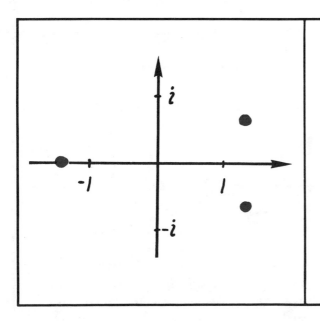

**1.5.4.** Again, the spectrum of the combined saddle point is the union of the spectra of the components. The conjugate pair in the right half-plane is contributed by the spiral repellor in the outset. The other CE, on the negative real axis in the left half-plane, belongs to the one-dimensional attractor in the inset. Again, the number of CEs on the right equals the index of the combined critical point.

Excluding the degenerate cases with coincident CEs, six more typical hyperbolic critical points may be constructed in this way, for a total of eight. Again, a critical point is called *elementary* if it is hyperbolic, with distinct CEs.

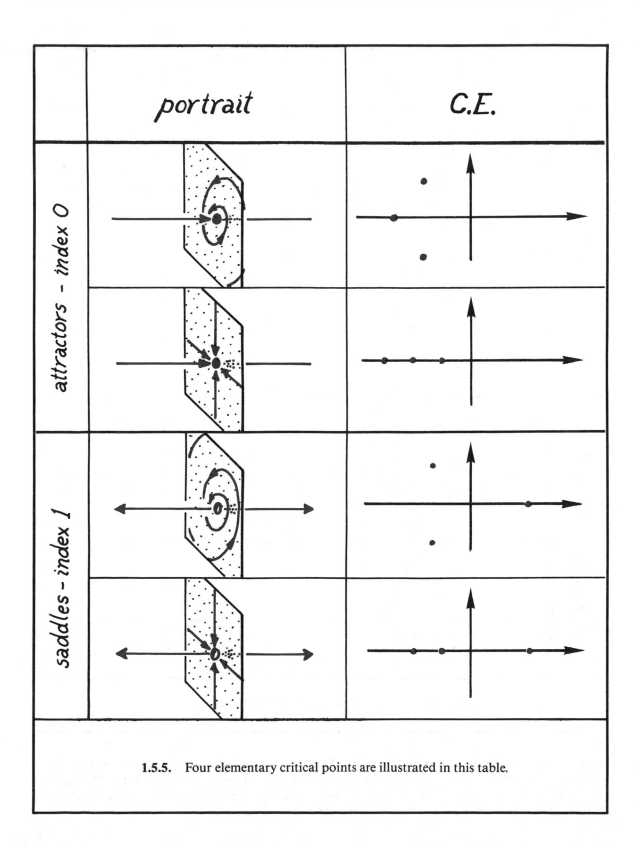

**1.5.5.** Four elementary critical points are illustrated in this table.

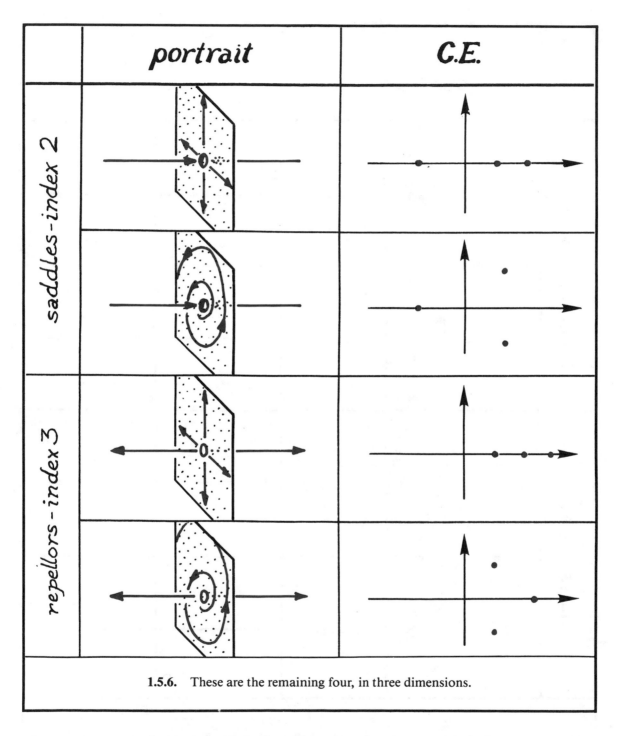

**1.5.6.** These are the remaining four, in three dimensions.

There are many more degenerate cases in three dimensions than in two. They include the hyperbolic cases with coincident CEs on the real axis. We have not illustrated any of these degenerate critical points, as they are exceptional. That is, they are rarely encountered in applications, except in the context of *bifurcations,* described in *Part Four* of this series.

## 2.  Periodic Limit Sets and Characteristic Multipliers

We have encountered periodic limit sets, or *limit cycles,* in most of the examples in *Part One.* In this chapter we will review the typical ones which occur in dimensions two and three. Also, within this review, we will add an important concept, the *Poincaré characteristic multipliers,* or CMs, of these limit cycles. Like the CEs of critical points, these characterize the geometry of the insets and outsets of typical limit cycles.

## 2.1. LIMIT CYCLES IN THE PLANE

In *Part One,* we described eight exemplary dynamical systems, five of them with planar state spaces. We now recall the two kinds of limit cycles occurring among them, and describe their CMs. In this context, each limit cycle has a single CM. In general, the number of CMs is one less than the dimension of the state space.

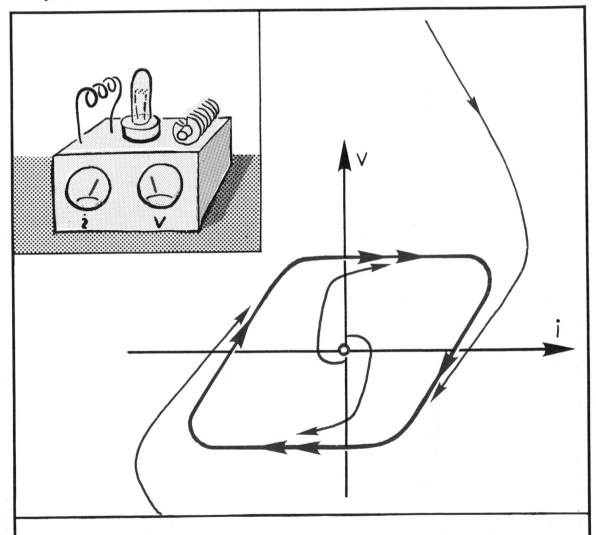

**2.1.1.** Van der Pol's dynamical model for the radio transmitter contains one limit cycle, which is attractive. It is a *periodic attractor.* All other trajectories (other than the critical point at the origin) tend asymptotically to this limit cycle.

**There is no obvious way to define CEs for this limit set. We will describe a subtle way, due to Poincaré.**

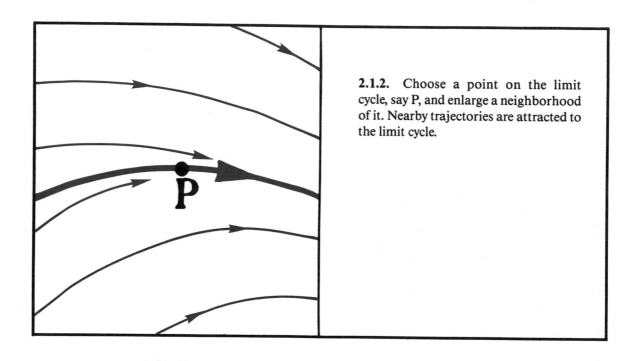

**2.1.2.** Choose a point on the limit cycle, say P, and enlarge a neighborhood of it. Nearby trajectories are attracted to the limit cycle.

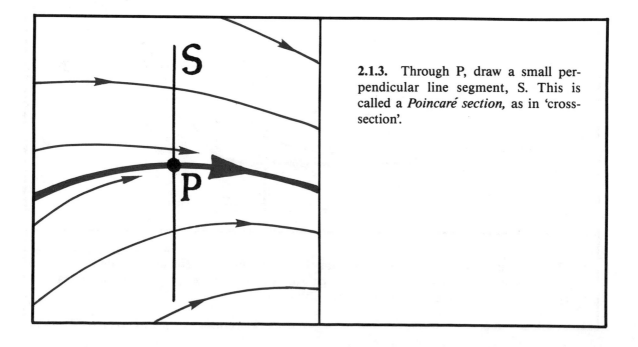

**2.1.3.** Through P, draw a small perpendicular line segment, S. This is called a *Poincaré section,* as in 'cross-section'.

**2.1.4.** Start at a point in S above P, say x, and follow its trajectory, determined by the dynamical system of Van der Pol. This trajectory follows around near the limit cycle. Eventually, it passes through the section again. Let R(x) denote the first return of the trajectory of x to S. This point, R(x), is above P in S, but is closer to P than x is, as the limit cycle is attractive. Starting at a point y of S below P, say y, the first return of the trajectory of y to S, R(y), is below P, but closer than is y. Likewise, every point of S has a first return to S. This defines a function from S to itself called the *first return map*, R. Note that R(P) = P.

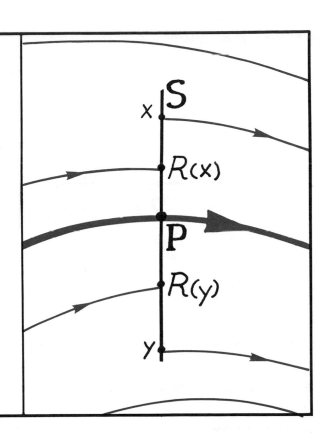

**2.1.5.** Make a square with the line segment, S, for each side. The graph of R is a curve in this square. It passes through (P,P) because R(P) = P.

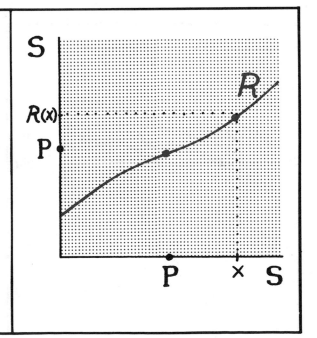

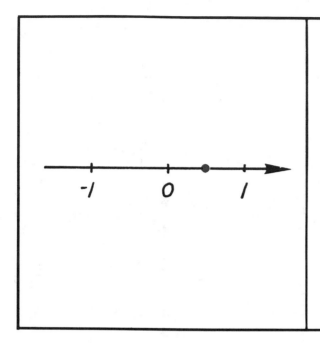

**2.1.6.** The CM is defined as the slope of this curve over the point P of S. This is necessarily a positive real number, in this context. For example if its about 1/2, as shown in this example (2.1.4), then R(x) will be about half as far from P as is x. The limit cycle must be an attractor.

For the limit cycle of the Van der Pol system, the CM is between zero and one because the limit cycle is attractive.

**Let's consider another system in the plane, with a periodic repellor. The CM of a periodic repellor in the plane is a real number greater than one.**

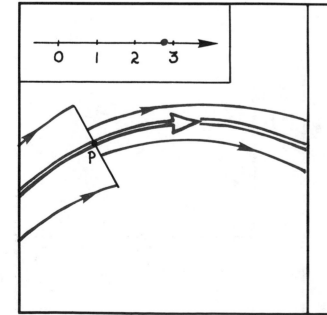

**2.1.7.** For example, if the CM is about three, as shown here, then R(x) will be about three times as far from P as is x. Thus, the limit cycle must be a repellor.

A limit cycle in the plane is called *hyperbolic* if its CM is not equal to one. There are only two cases. A periodic attractor has its CM between zero and one, while a periodic repellor has its CM greater than one. A limit cycle with CM equal to one may be *neither* an attractor nor a repellor.

**What causes the CM to be *equal* to one?**

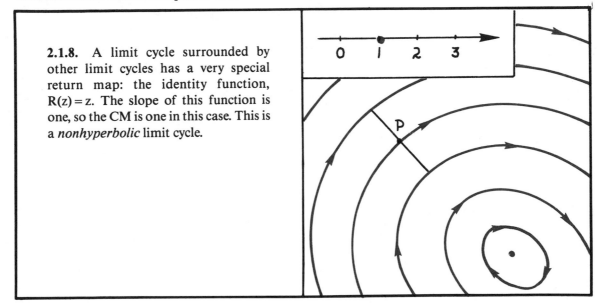

**2.1.8.** A limit cycle surrounded by other limit cycles has a very special return map: the identity function, $R(z) = z$. The slope of this function is one, so the CM is one in this case. This is a *nonhyperbolic* limit cycle.

**Recall the frictionless pendulum, panel 2.1.18 of *Part One*. This is an example of a nonhyperbolic limit cycle.**

## 2.2.  LIMIT CYCLES IN A MÖBIUS BAND

In the preceding section, we found that the CM of a limit cycle in the plane was inevitably a positive real number. Why do we never come across a negative CM? The answer is: we do! But only in a non-orientable surface, as we shall see in this section.

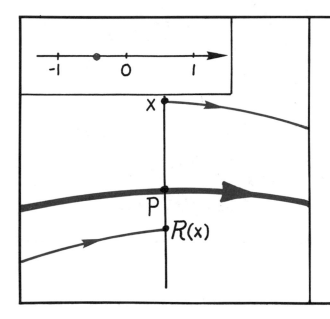

**2.2.1.**  Suppose we have zoomed-in on a Poincaré section of a limit cycle in a two-dimensional context, graphed the return map, and found a *negative* slope, or CM. Then necessarily, a point in the section above the cycle, like x here, has a first return on the *opposite side* of the cycle, like R(x) here.

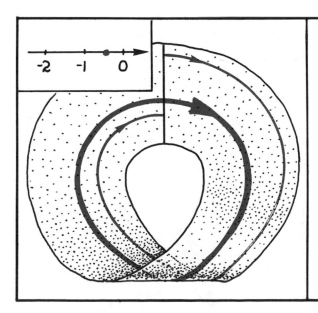

**2.2.2.**  Now let's zoom back out, so we can see the entire limit cycle, and the entire trajectory from x to R(x). There has to be a *twist* in the surface, in order for the return map to *reverse orientation* of the Poincaré section. The Möbius band, shown here, is just one of the many possibilities.

**The CM of a periodic attractor around a Möbius band is a negative real number, between −1 and 0.**

**2.2.3.** A periodic repellor around a Möbius band has a CM less than −1.

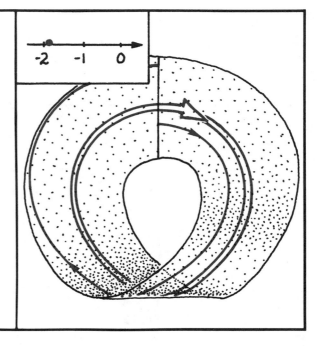

**2.2.4.** A limit cycle around a Möbius band with a CM equal to −1 is non-hyperbolic. In this case, the limit cycle belongs to a family of "parallel" periodic trajectories.

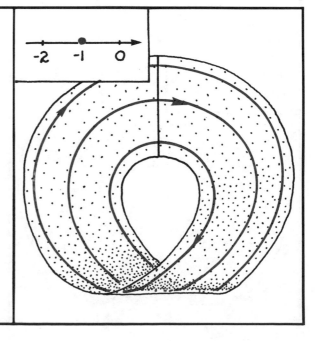

**Of course, not all limit cycles in a Möbius band have negative CMs.**

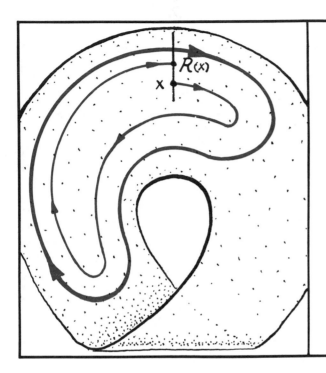

**2.2.5.** For example, a limit cycle which does not go all the way around...

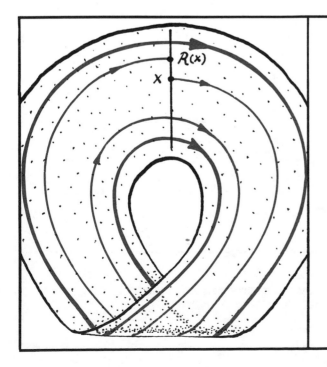

**2.2.6.** . . . or one which goes twice around.

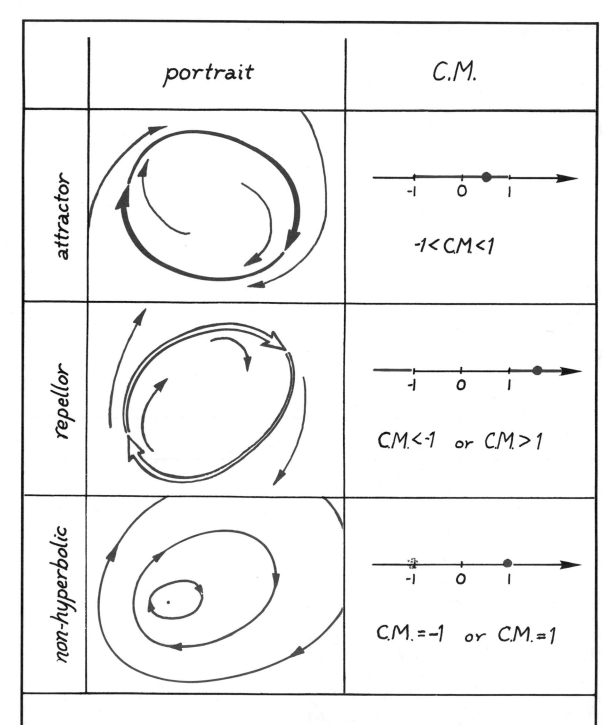

**2.2.7.** The limit cycles in two-dimensional state spaces are classified in this table, which includes both positive and negative CM contexts. The CM is never zero.

## 2.3. SADDLE CYCLES IN THREE DIMENSIONS

In two-dimensional state spaces, typical limit cycles are either attractors or repellors. In three-dimensional contexts, there are several possibilities.

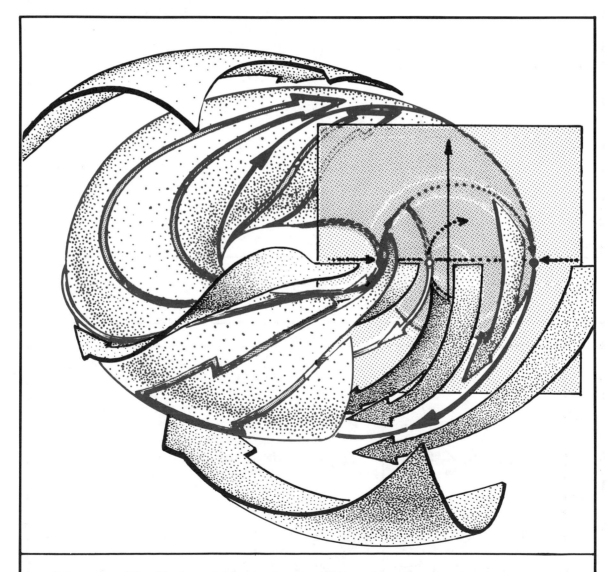

**2.3.1.** Recall Duffing's model for the forced pendulum, from *Part One,* Panel 5.4.12. There are three prominent limit cycles in a three-dimensional context: an attractor, a saddle, and a repellor.

Now we are going to characterize these limit cycles in terms of the CMs of Poincaré. His subtle construction of the CMs of a limit cycle works in contexts of any dimension.

**We will consider the saddle cycle first.**

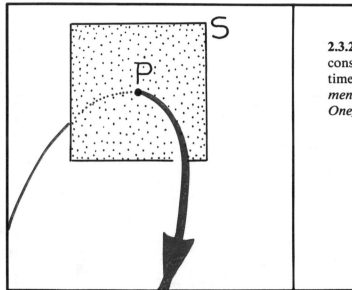

**2.3.2.** At a point, P, in the limit cycle, construct a small cross-section, S. This time, the Poincare section is *two-dimensional,* like the *strobe planes* of *Part One,* Chapter 4.

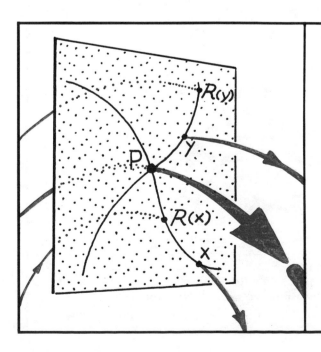

**2.3.3.** Each point of S (if it's not too close to the edge, at least), when prolonged forward along its trajectory, will have a first return to the section. Here, the point x returns at R(x), while another point y returns at R(y). As x is chosen here in the *inset,* R(x) is closer to the limit cycle. On the other hand, y is in the *outset,* so R(y) is farther from the limit cycle.

This construction defines a function from (most of) S to itself, the *first return map,* R. The graph of R is a surface in four-space, so we cannot draw it pictorially. But according to vector calculus, as described in *Volume Zero* of this Series, R may be approximated very well, in a neighborhood of P, by a linear transformation. The theory of these, linear algebra, provides an algorithm for obtaining two complex numbers, the *eigenvalues* of this linear approximation. These characterize the linear transformation exactly, and the first return map approximately. These two complex numbers are, in general, either real, or a complex conjugate pair. *These are the CMs of the limit cycle.*

**2.3.4.** In the case of the saddle cycle in Duffing's system, the CMs are positive real numbers. One is *larger* than one, characterizing the *outset.* The other is *smaller* than one, characterizing the *inset.*

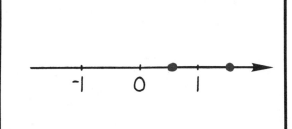

**2.3.5.** The curve in S corresponding to the smaller CM (shown in the box) is the cross-section of the *inset* of the limit cycle. This surface is *invariant:* trajectories which start on it, stay on it. Within this invariant surface, the inset, the limit cycle acts as an attractor. The smaller CM determines the rate of this attraction. The smaller the CM, the faster the asymptotic approach to the limit cycle.

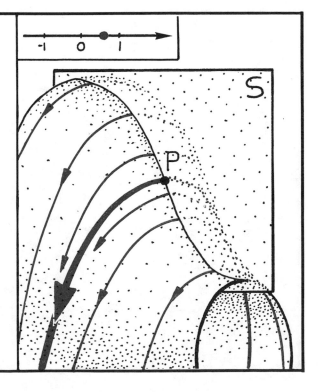

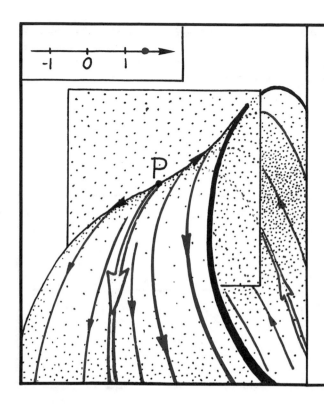

**2.3.6.** The other curve in S, corresponding to the larger CM (see below), is the cross-section of the *outset* of the limit cycle. Within this invariant surface, the limit cycle acts as a repellor. The larger the CM, the stronger this repulsion.

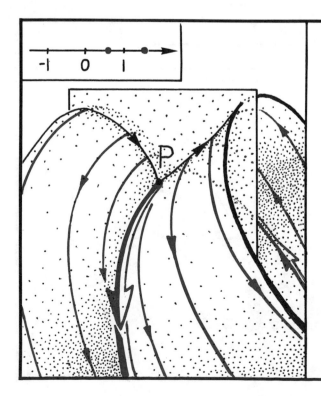

**2.3.7.** Here are the two invariant surfaces, inset and outset. They intersect in a curve, the limit cycle. Only small portions of them are shown here. They both may extend far out of the picture. Both CMs are shown in the box.

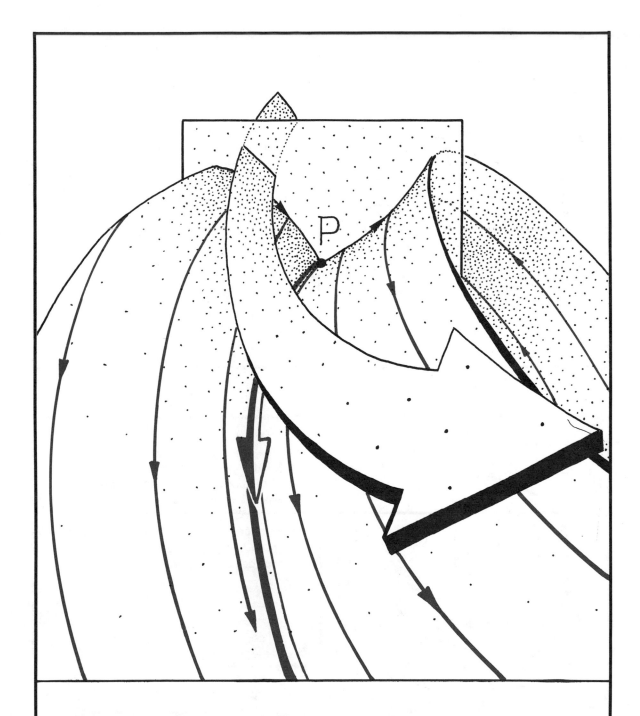

**2.3.8.** The trajectories of the inset spiral toward the limit cycle, while those of the outset spiral away. Other nearby trajectories just fly on by, spiraling closer for a while, then spiraling away.

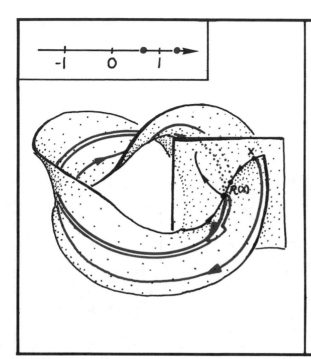

**2.3.9.** Even though the CMs are positive, the inset and outset cylinders may be twisted. But they must twist an *even* number of twists, if the CMs are *positive*. Here, for better visibility, we have shown only the inset.

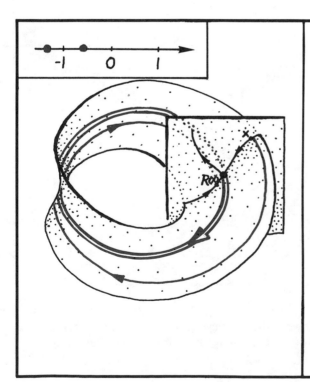

**2.3.10.** As in the two-dimensional case of the preceding section, *negative* CMs arise when both the inset and the outset are Möbius bands, each with an *odd* number of twists while going once around. Again, the outset band has been deleted for better visibility.

## 2.4. NODAL CYCLES IN THREE DIMENSIONS

Here we consider variations on the saddle cycle of the preceding section. If the CMs are real and both small (between $-1$ and 1) we have an attracting or repelling cycle which looks rather like a saddle. These are called *nodal cycles*.

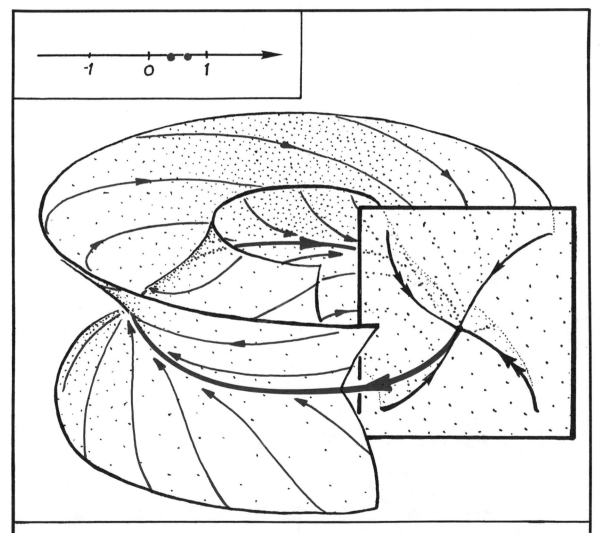

**2.4.1.** These two small, real CMs correspond to two invariant surfaces, as in the saddle cycle. But the limit cycle acts as an attractor within each. One, with the smaller CM, attracts more strongly than the other. They are *sub-insets,* called the *fast-inset* and the *slow-inset* respectively.

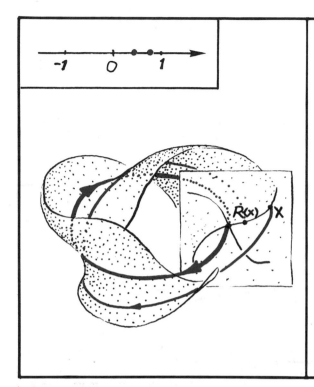

**2.4.2.** As with saddle cycles, these *positive* CMs could correspond to surfaces with any *even* number of twists. Here, the first return, R(x), is on the *same* side of the fast-inset as the initial point, x.

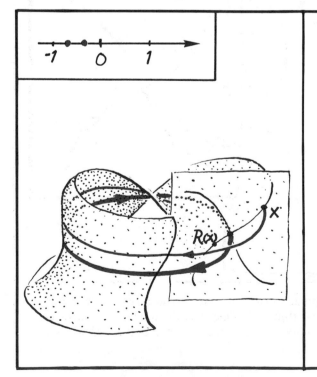

**2.4.3.** And as with saddle cycles, the invariant surfaces may both be twisted an *odd* number of times. In this case, the CMs are *negative,* and the first return, R(x), is on the *opposite* side from the initial point, x.

**2.4.4.** Repelling cycles can be nodal, too. Here, the two large (greater than one), real CMs correspond to two invariant surfaces, the fast- and slow-outsets. But the limit cycle acts as a repellor within each.

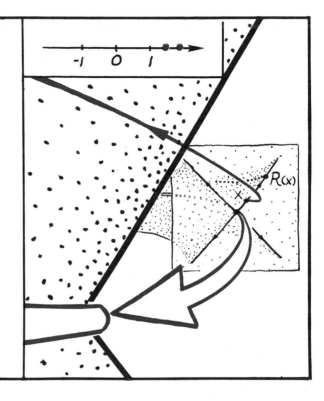

**2.4.5.** Repelling nodal cycles may also have twisted fast and slow-outsets, with negative CMs.

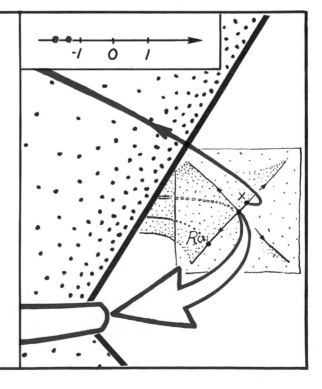

## 2.5.  SPIRAL CYCLES IN THREE DIMENSIONS

As the two CMs of a limit cycle in three space are the eigenvalues of a linear transformation, it is possible for them to be a pair of conjugate complex numbers, rather than a pair of real numbers. This is the case with limit cycles of spiral type.

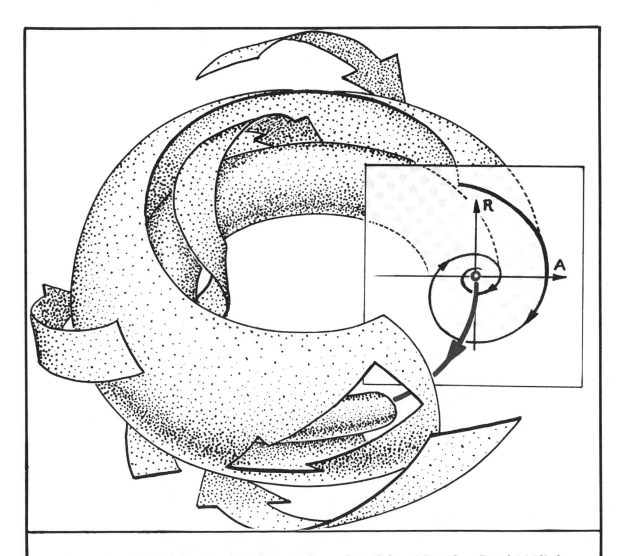

**2.5.1.**   Recall that in the ring model for the damped pendulum ( *Part One,* Panel 4.1.12) the periodic attractor around the center was surrounded by spiraling trajectories.

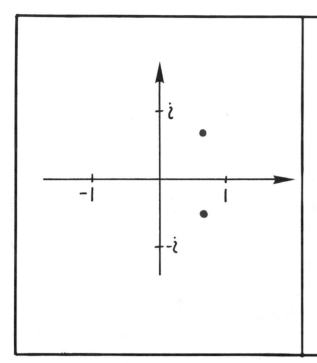

**2.5.2.** Since there are no invariant sur-faces as in the case of a nodal cycle, the CMs cannot be real. They are a conju-gate pair of complex numbers. The *magnitude* (distance of either from the origin) characterizes the rate of asymp-totic approach to the limit cycle. The *angle* (in the sense of polar coordinates) characterizes the rate of spiraling.

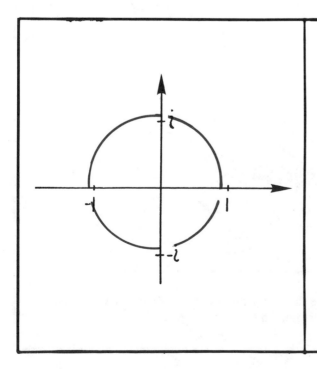

**2.5.3.** The unit circle in the complex plane discriminates attractors from re-pellors.

**2.5.4.** In the case of a spiral *attractor,* the complex conjugate CMs are *inside* the unit circle.

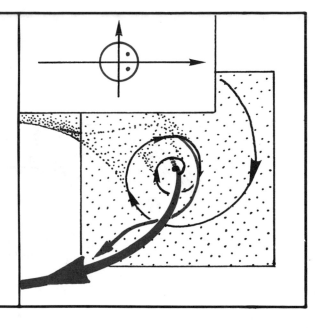

**2.5.5.** In the case of a spiral *repellor,* the complex conjugate CMs are *outside* the unit circle.

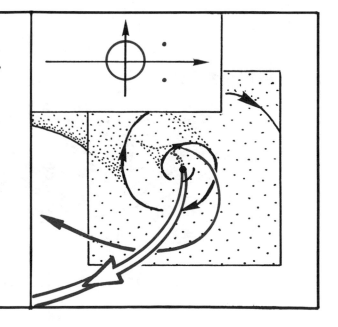

**What about CMs *on* the unit circle?**

**A limit cycle is** *hyperbolic* if none of its CMs are on the unit circle. An important example of a non-hyperbolic limit cycle in three-space is a *center.*

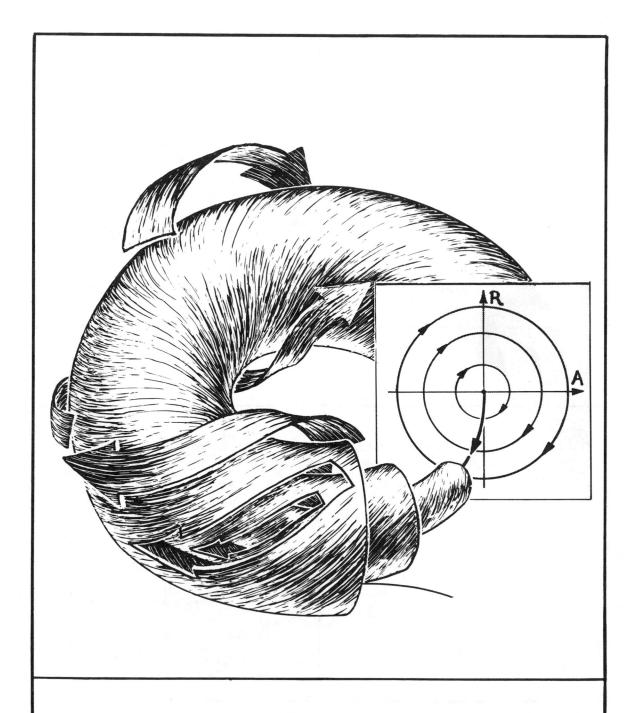

**2.5.6.** A center is surrounded by concentric tori, which are invariant surfaces. Nearby trajectories stay on these tori, neither attracted nor repelled by the central limit cycle.

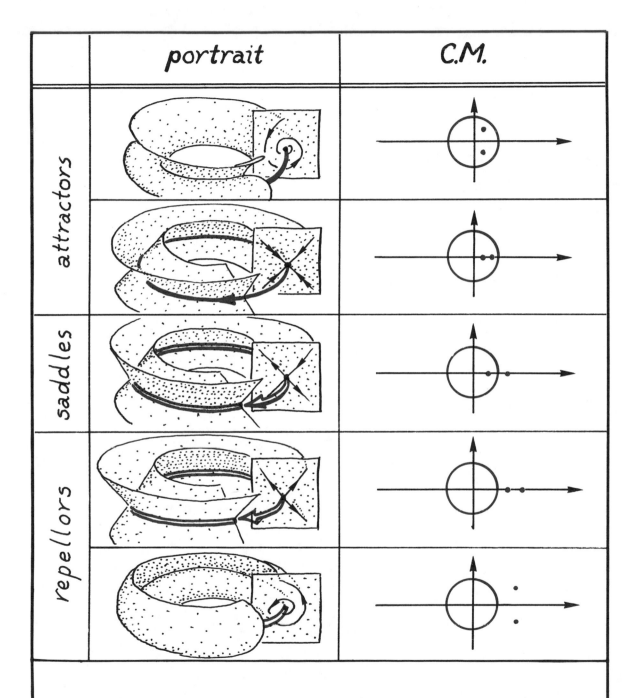

**2.5.7.** A limit cycle is called *elementary* if it is hyperbolic, and its CMs are distinct (no two equal). All the elementary limit cycles in three space are summarized in this table.

## 2.6.    CHARACTERISTIC EXPONENTS

In the case of a limit *point,* the local asymptotic behavior is described by the CEs. The number of CEs is equal to the dimension of the state space. In the case of a limit *cycle,* the local asymptotic behavior is described by the CMs. The number of CMs is equal to the dimension of the Poincaré section, one less than the dimension of the state space.

**In this section, we develop the relationship between CEs and CMs.**

**2.6.1.** Recall, from the preceding Chapter, that with CEs, the *horizontal coordinate* (real) indicates the strength of repulsion (right half) or attraction (left half). The *vertical coordinate* (imaginary) indicates the rate of spiraling. The CEs on the left are *attractive.* Those on the right are *repulsive.* The imaginary axis is excluded, for hyperbolic limit points. We will call this diagram the *CE plane.*

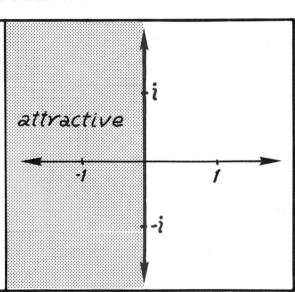

**2.6.2.** On the other hand, in the preceding Section, we have seen that, with CMs, the *magnitude* indicates strength of repulsion, while the *angle* characterizes spiraling. The CMs are *attractive* if inside the unit circle, and *repulsive* when outside. The unit circle is excluded for hyperbolic limit cycles. We will call this diagram the *CM plane.*

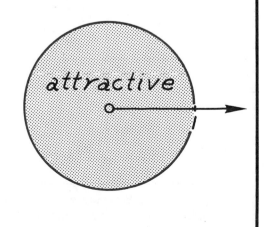

We now describe a function from the CE plane to the CM plane, called the *exponential map,* or *polar coordinates.*

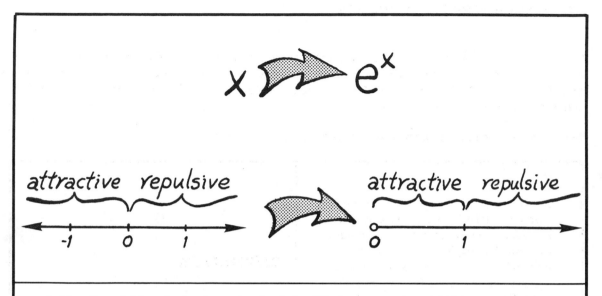

**2.6.3.** *Step 1.* Map the horizontal axis of the CE plane onto the positive half of the horizontal axis of the CM plane, using the natural exponental function. Note that *zero is mapped to one.*

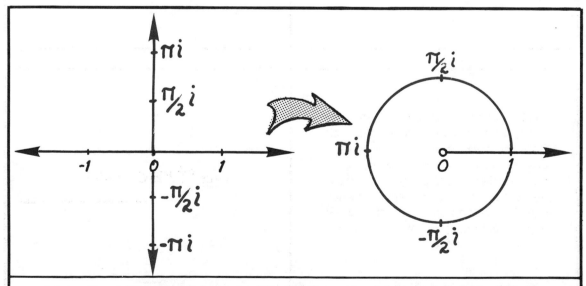

**2.6.4.** *Step 2.* Wrap the vertical axis of the CE plane around the unit circle of the CM plane. *Linear measure* on the real axis of the CE plane becomes *angular measure* on the unit circle of the CM plane.

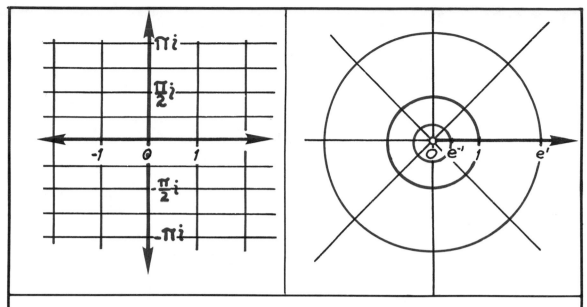

**2.6.5.** *Step 3. Horizontal lines* in the CE plane are mapped into *rays* in the CM plane, radiating from the origin. *Vertical lines* in the CE plane are wrapped around *concentric circles* in the CM plane. No point in the CE plane goes to the origin of the CM plane.

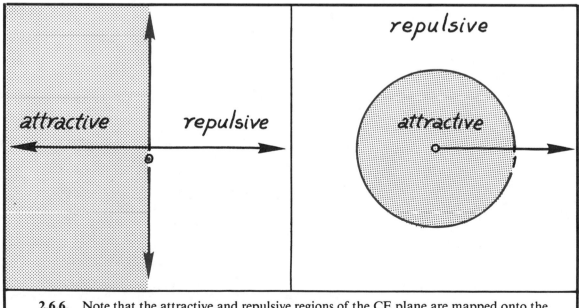

**2.6.6.** Note that the attractive and repulsive regions of the CE plane are mapped onto the corresponding regions of the CM plane.

We could use this mapping to define CEs for limit cycles, but this will not be necessary.

## 2.7. DISCRETE POWER SPECTRA

Before ending this review and expansion of *Part One,* we pause to emphasize the periodic attributes of attractive limit cycles. This explains why we call them *periodic attractors,* which is not because they come and go!

**2.7.1.** In *Part One,* Panels 2.3.5 to 2.3.7, we discussed the pitch and volume of *pure tones.* These are attributes of *sinusoidal time series,* or time records of one coordinate of a *regular* (circular) periodic attractor.

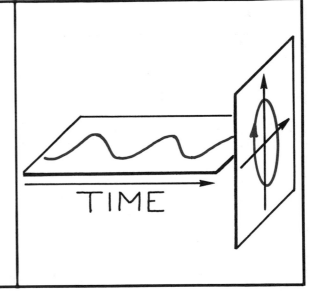

**2.7.2.** A time series from another, very *irregular,* periodic attractor might look like this. It may be *bumpy,* but it is *periodic* in the sense that the same irregular pattern is repeated over and over. Each repetition takes the same period of time —hence *periodic. The reciprocal* of the period of time is the *frequency* of the periodic time series. This one would sound like a complex tone, with a colorful timbre.

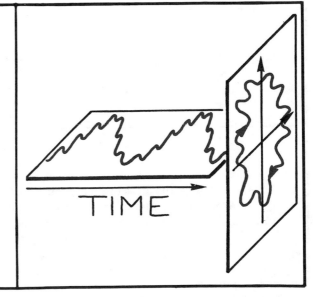

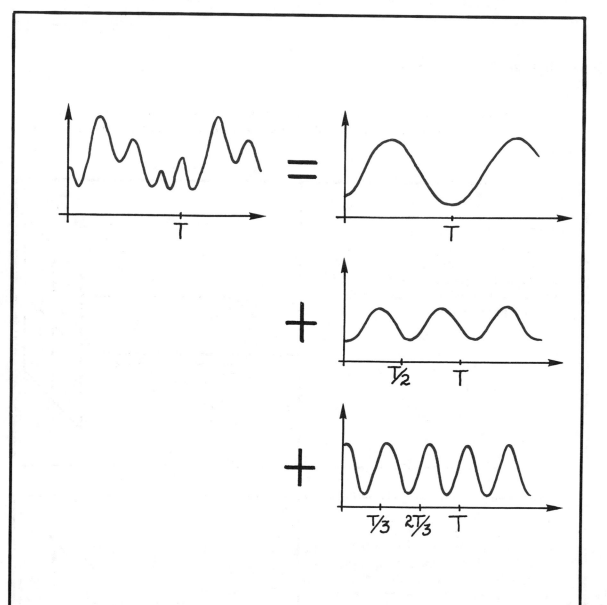

**2.7.3.**   Following the ideas of Fourier analysis, we may represent the irregular periodic time series (or tone) as a sum of regular (sinusoidal) pure tones of various frequencies, amplitudes, and relative phases, all sounded together.

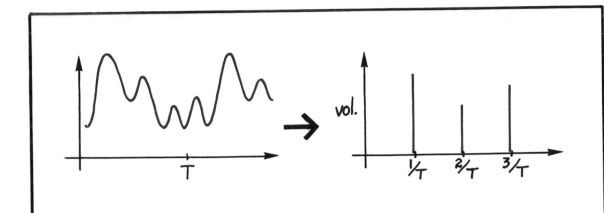

**2.7.4.** Recording the square of the amplitude, and the frequency, of each of the component pure tones in a diagram such as this is called the *power spectrum* of the periodic time series (complex tone). In this case, the power spectrum is *discrete,* as it consists of discrete vertical line segments. This is characteristic of periodic attractors.

Likewise, continuous power spectra are uncharacteristic of periodic attractors. And yet, they abound in music, and throughout nature, in *noise*. The dynamical model for a noisy time series is the chaotic attractor, to which we turn at last.

# 3.   Chaotic Limit Sets

Points and cycles are not the only limit sets found in dynamical systems. The torus is a limit set proved to be rare in theory, but frequently seen in experiments. Reasons are given in *Part Three, Stable Behavior.* In this chapter, we introduce some of the curious limit sets discovered by experimentalists. Among all kinds of limit sets, only the attractors are directly observable in simulations by analog and digital computers. So this chapter will emphasize chaotic attractors, primarily. The reasons these are called *chaotic* will be described in the last chapter.

### 3.1.  POINCARÉ'S SOLENOID

Poincaré's discovery of *homoclinic tangles,* and their subsequent analysis by Birkhoff and Smale, are described in detail in *Part Three* of this series. Poincaré predicted, in his original description of homoclinic tangles, that they might be too complicated ever to be understood. The full picture, recently emerged, contains a chaotic limit set of saddle type, which we call *Poincaré's solenoid.* In this section, we describe the superficial appearance of this theoretical object.

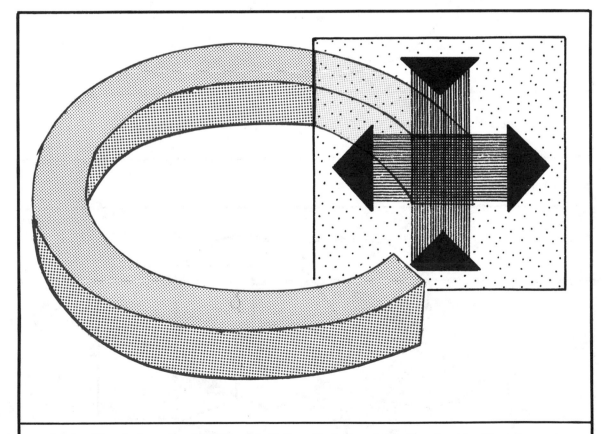

**3.1.1.** Here is the solenoid. Like an infinite coil of wire, shown here in red with a piece cut away for visibility, it might be regarded as a thickening of a periodic trajectory of saddle type. But, it has an infinite number of pieces, as we shall see. In this representation, we emphasize its Poincaré cross-section. The inset cross-section is a thickened curve, with an infinite number of pieces. The outset cross-section is also a thickened curve.

**Let's build up this picture, piece by piece.**

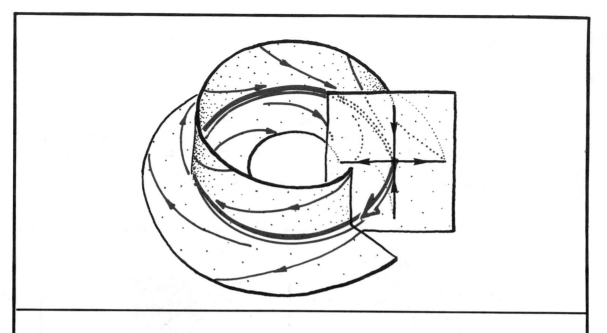

**3.1.2.**   Recall, from Section 2.3, this typical periodic saddle in three-space.

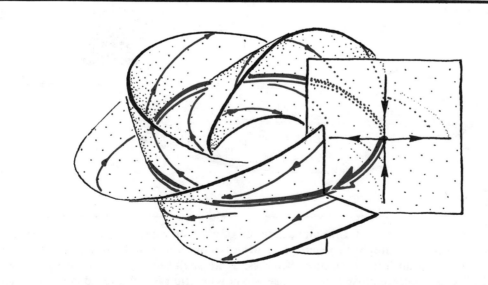

**3.1.3.**   This twisted version has Möbius bands for its inset and outset. Each has a single twist.

Next, consider a twisted periodic saddle going *twice around* before closing. Each half almost closes, but not quite. The inset of each half is twisted, like a Möbius band. These half-insets may thus be parallel, without crossing. The outset of each half is likewise twisted, so these may be parallel as well. We may visualize this as follows.

**3.1.4.** Take a narrow strip of paper (1) and fold it the long way (2).

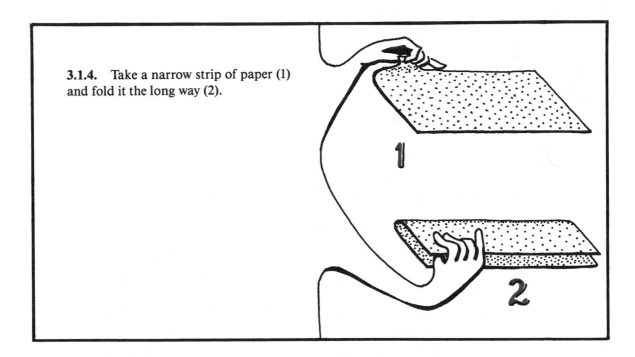

**3.1.5.** Use this folded strip to make a Möbius band, twisting and taping carefully (3). Note that the fold does not match up at the taped part. This is no problem, because we...

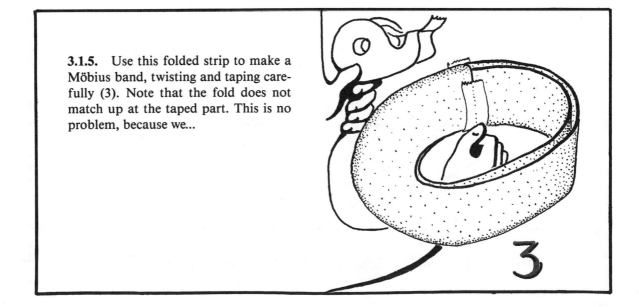

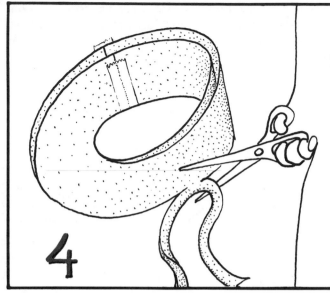

**3.1.6.** What remains is a double strip. This is the *inset-model.*

4

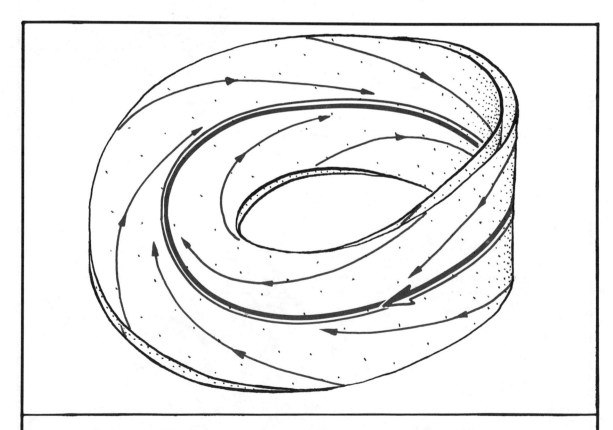

**3.1.7.** Here is the inset model, with the limit cycle and the attracted trajectories drawn on it.

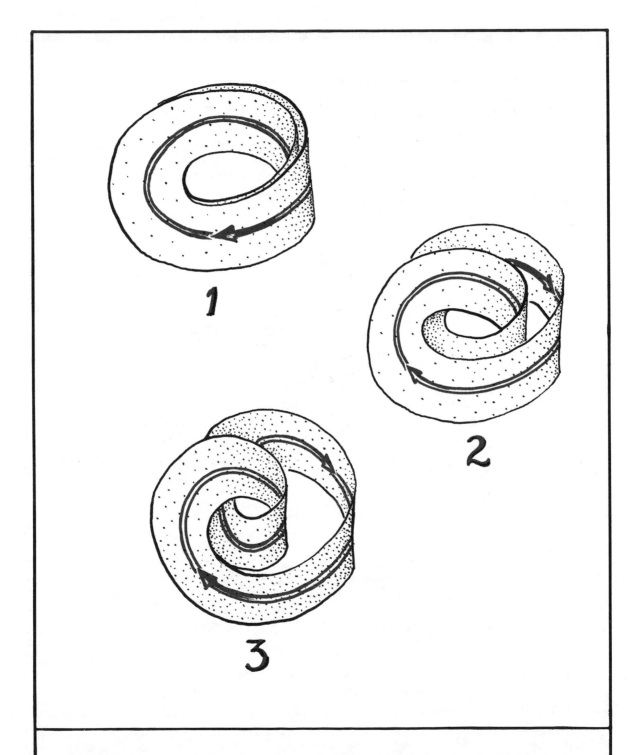

**3.1.8.** Trying to uncoil the inset model, we find that we have a long band, which is *double twisted*.

Now take another narrow strip of paper. Fold, twist, and tape, as above, but with this complementary orientation.

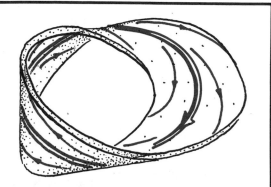

**3.1.9.** This model is horizontal where the previous one was vertical, and so on. Cutting off the fold, we obtain this model for the outset of our double periodic trajectory. This is the *outset-model*.

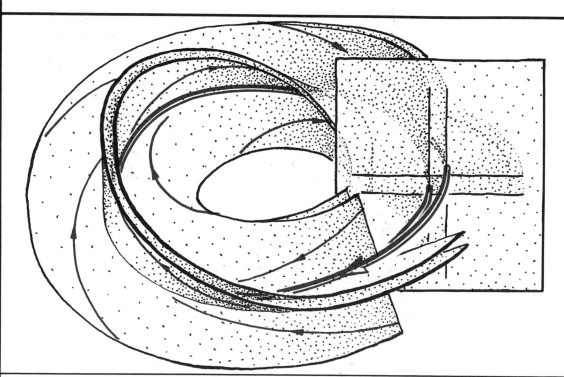

**3.1.10.** Putting together the two models, we obtain this picture of the double periodic trajectory. The trajectory completes two revolutions before closing, likewise the inset and outset bands.

Note that the inset and outset *must intersect* in this picture. The intersection is another saddle cycle which completes two revolutions before closing. The outset of the new cycle coincides with the inset of the original one, and *vice versa*. This is the complication Poincaré had noticed and despaired. The fantastic consequence of this intersection, obtained by a small perturbation, is known as a *homoclinic tangle*. This is detailed in *Part Three, Stable Behavior*. For the present, we will ignore this consequence.

**3.1.11.** We could equally well *fold the strip twice,* like this.

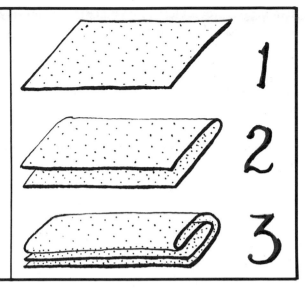

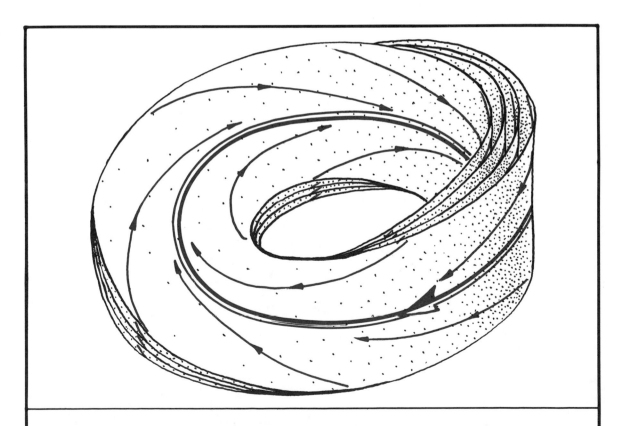

**3.1.12.** Twisting, taping, and cutting, we obtain an inset-model for a quadruple periodic trajectory.

Iterating this procedure, we may make models for very long periodic trajectories, all coiled so as to fit in the same ring. All these may have their insets parallel, likewise their outsets. Adding trajectories which coil around the ring endlessly *without closing,* we obtain a complicated limit set of saddle type, Poincaré's solenoid, as shown in panel 3.1.1. The occurrence of this limit set in the forced Van der Pol system (*Part One, Periodic Behavior,* Ch. 5) was suggested by Cartwright and Littlewood, and fully analyzed by Smale, as explained in the Hall of Fame. It is not observed in experiments, because it is *not an attractor.*

**We turn now to the chaotic limit sets which are actually attractive.**

## 3.2.   BIRKHOFF'S BAGEL

Birkhoff picked up dynamical systems theory, in 1912, where it was left by Poincaré's death. Within four years, he had discovered the chaotic attractor, as a theoretical object in discrete dynamical systems (1932). This was his *remarkable curve,* found in the dynamics of a map of the plane to itself. This was later studied by Charpentier (1935), and is still an active research topic. This so-called curve is actually thicker than a normal one-dimensional curve, so we call it a *thick curve.* Thickness, in this sense, relates to *fractal dimension,* explained in the next chapter.

In 1944, Levinson raised the question of the occurrence of this attractor in the context of forced oscillation. Here, the plane would be the strobe plane, a Poincaré section, and the map of the plane to itself would be the first return map. Then the remarkable (thick) curve of Birkhoff would be the strobe section of a thick torus, which we call here a *bagel.* He answered this question in the affirmative for a particular system, similar to the forced Van der Pol (1948, 1949).

Meanwhile, Cartwright and Littlewood announced a similar result (1945) for the forced Van der Pol system, and later published their proof (1949). They pointed out experimental evidence for this strange attractor, which they had found in the earliest electronic simulations of the Van der Pol system, done by Van der Pol himself in collaboration with Van der Mark (1927).

Recent experiments by Holmes (1977) on the Duffing system, and by R. Shaw (1980) on the forced Van der Pol system (standard and variations) with an analog computer have detailed the folded structure of Birkhoff's attractor, which we present in this section. Our presentation relies heavily on *Part One* of this Series.

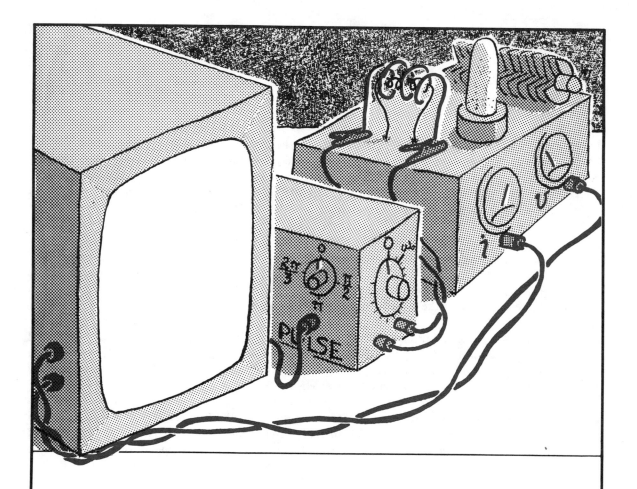

**3.2.1.** Recall that Van der Pol studied forced oscillators in the context of radio transmitters and receivers. Here is the analog device, as explained in *Part One,* Chapter 5. The transmitter (right) is forced by an isolated oscillator (center). Its plate voltage and current are monitored by a storage scope (left) only during a short pulse sent by the forcing oscillator. This strobe pulse is in phase with the forcing oscillation. Here we have added a control knob to the forcing oscillator (shown high on its left side). This is for changing the phase of the forcing oscillation at which the strobe pulse is sent.

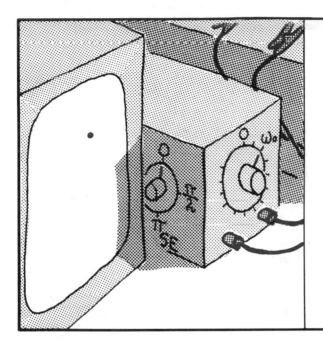

**3.2.2.** With the frequency of the forcing oscillator close to the natural frequency of the unforced radio oscillator, the combined system may oscillate in an *isochronous harmonic*. In this case, we observe a single dot on the storage scope, shown here in red.

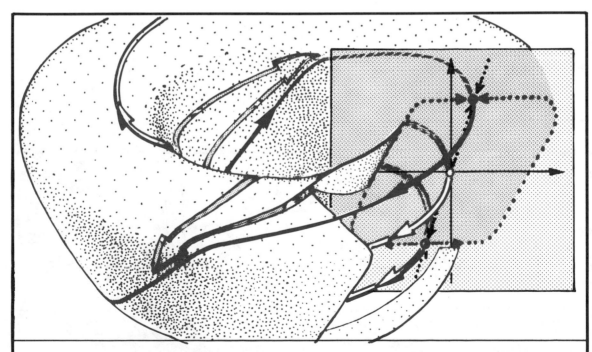

**3.2.3.** Advancing the phase control from phase zero forwards to phase 2π, we see the dot advance around a closed loop. Assembling these planar sections in the three-dimensional state space of the ring model (see Chapter 5 of *Part One, Periodic Behavior,* we see the isochronous harmonic as a periodic trajectory on an attractive invariant torus.

**By increasing the frequency of the driving oscillator, we may observe many different braids, as described in *Part One*, Chapter 5.**

**3.2.4.** For example, an ultraharmonic would appear, in the strobe plane or storage scope screen, as a discrete point set on the section of the invariant torus. With each pulse from the forcing oscillator, one of the dots is refreshed. In other words, the trajectory hits the strobe plane repeatedly. The successive hits cycle through the discrete point set, repeatedly. The order of successive hits is not simply clockwise, or counter-clockwise. However, the same order is repeated each cycle. Thus, if we watch for a while, we learn to predict the next hit exactly.

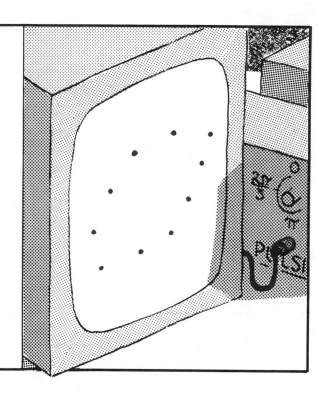

**3.2.5.** For some higher frequency, and carefully chosen amplitude, we find what appears to be a continuous closed curve, instead of a discrete point set. This is the *remarkable curve of Birkhoff,* exactly as predicted by Levinson. As far as we know, this was not actually observed until very recently (R. Shaw, 1980). The trajectory hits the strobe plane in a point which appears to rove randomly around this curve. Unlike the preceding (periodic) situation, we find ourselves unable to predict the next hit of the trajectory on the strange curve, no matter how long we observe it.

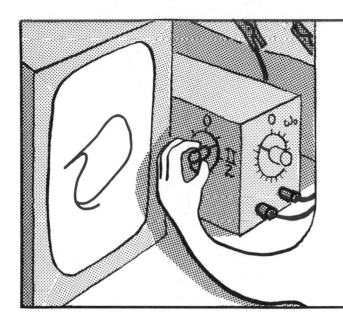

**3.2.6.** Adjusting the phase control reveals a rotating distortion of the closed curve. The spike slowly crawls to the right along the top, while the lower spurs march briskly to the left along the bottom. One by one, they catch up with the upper spike, and merge with it.

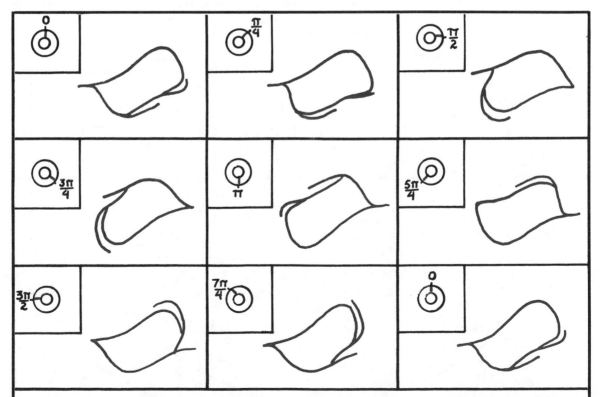

**3.2.7.** Here is a sequence of eight successive phases, a full cycle around the ring model, exactly as discovered by Robert Shaw (1980) in analog simulation of Van der Pol's system. His equations are reproduced in the Appendix.

**3.2.8.** Assembling Robert Shaw's sections in the ring model for the forced Van der Pol system, the bagel emerges.

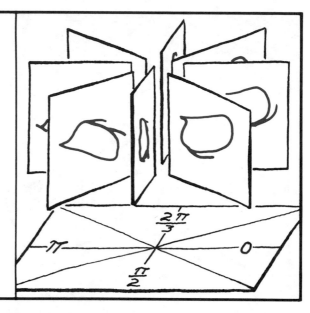

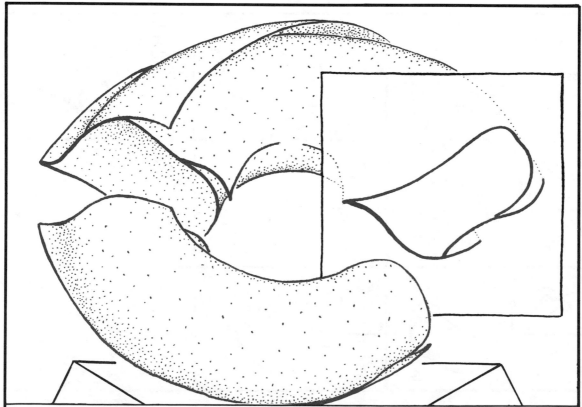

**3.2.9.** Interpolating more sections and smoothing between them, we obtain this folded, thickened surface. But this is essentially the trace of a *single trajectory. It is not a periodic trajectory.* The missing sections have been cut away for better visibility.

**This single trajectory represents a most irregular behavior of the forced oscillator,** *chaotic behavior.*

Let's color the bagel red. Now we isolate a small piece on Birkoff's remarkable curve, color it black, and follow it once around the bagel.

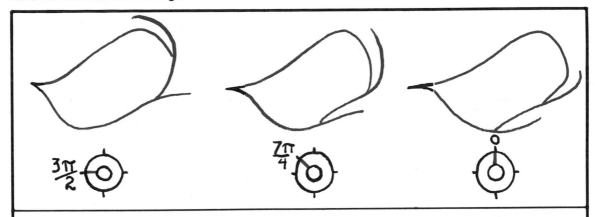

**3.2.10.**   Starting at phase $3\pi/2$, this black piece is pinched to a beak, and pulled out to the left, away from the main body of the bagel. It is not yet moving. But the two lower spurs (red) are moving down and to the left.

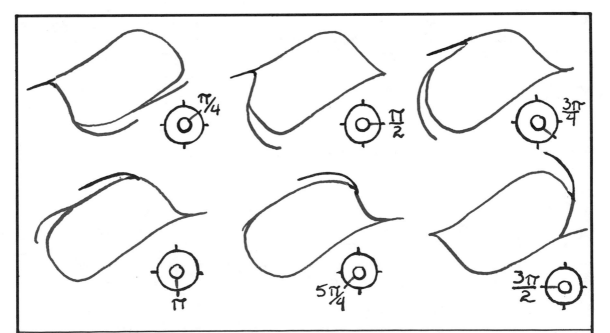

**3.2.11.**   After phase 0, the black beak is pinched more, elongates further, and crawls to the right along the top of the bagel. Meanwhile, the lower spurs are marching briskly around after the beak. At $\pi/2$, one of them has caught up with the beak, and merged with it. A new beak is forming on the right. At $5\pi/4$, the second spur has also merged. The old beak is now a spur. Finally, the new beak is fully formed, and become a spur, while yet a new beak has been born on the left.

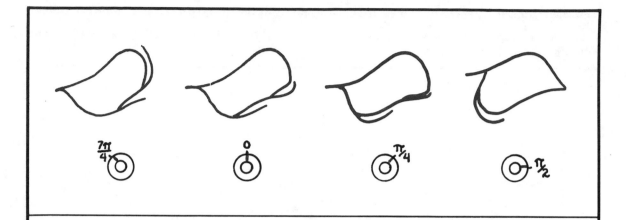

**3.2.12.**   Going on around a bit, the red spur is pressed flat into the side of the bagel, like a pleat. This whole process, from fresh beak to ironed pleat, took one and half cycles of the forcing oscillation.

The bagel consists of an infinite number of pleats, almost all of which have been pressed flat against the thickened toroid. This fractal microstructure, characteristic of all the known chaotic attractors, will be clarified in Chapter 4. It is actually responsible for their unpredictable behavior.

## 3.3. LORENZ'S MASK

The advent of digital computers made a great impact on dynamical systems theory. One of the early results was the surprising discovery, by Lorenz (1962, 1963), who had been a student of Birkhoff, of an unsuspected type of chaotic attractor. This discovery occurred during simulation of global weather patterns, and eventually provided science with its first deterministic model of *turbulence*.

**3.3.1.** The earth, warmed by the sun, heats the atmosphere from below, while outer space, always cold, absorbs heat from the outer shell of the atmosphere. The lower layer wants to rise, while the upper air wants to drop. This causes a traffic problem.

To visualize the air currents in the atmosphere, we construct a cross-section. The plane section, passing through the center of the earth, cuts the atmosphere in a ring. Let us look now at a small piece of that ring.

**3.3.2.** The traffic problem of the competing warm and cold air masses is solved by circulation vortices, called *Bénard cells.*

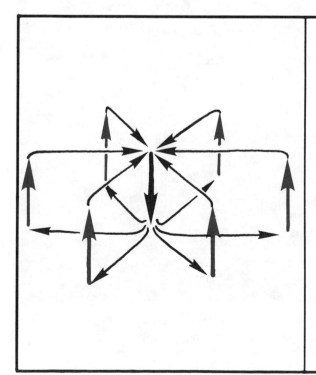

**3.3.3.** Returning to three dimensions, a typical vortex may have warm air rising in a ring, and cool air descending in the center like this.

**3.3.4.** The atmosphere, or at least a portion of its spherical shell perhaps as large as the Sahara Desert, might be seething in a sea of Bénard cells, closely packed as a hexagonal lattice.

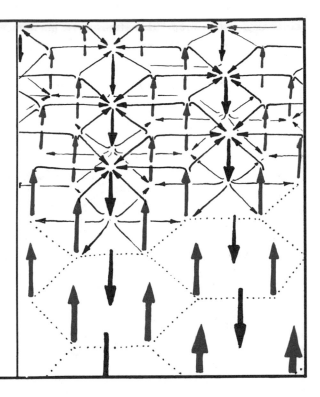

**3.3.5.** In fact, this aerial photo of the Sahara Desert shows, in the pattern of sand dunes, the sculptured footprint of such a sea of atmospheric vortices. Snowfields and icebergs reveal similar patterns, sculptured by invisible Bénard cells in the atmosphere.

**Lorenz set out to model this atmospheric phenomenon, using a dynamical system derived from the equations of fluid dynamics.**

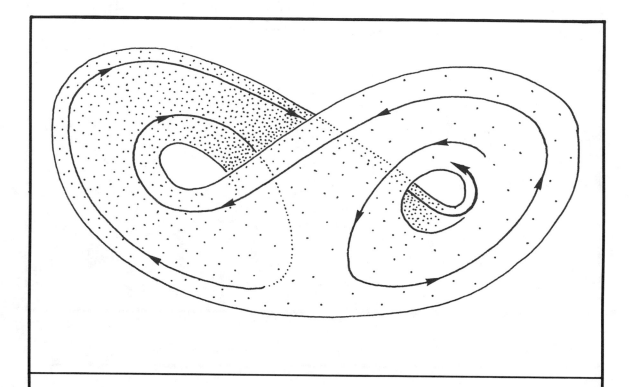

**3.3.6.**   Simulating the model with computer graphics in the early 1960's, he saw this on the screen. Here, as with the bagel in the preceding Section, the attracting object is rigidly determined. But the future of a trajectory within it is unpredictable by the observer. In the next Chapter, we will explain this paradox.

**Like Birkhoff's bagel, this is an attractor which is neither a point nor a cycle.**

The behavior of a trajectory following this attractor, as observed by Lorenz, is very erratic. It orbits one of the holes for a while, then jumps to the other for a while, and so on. This is why its behavior is called *chaotic,* as we shall see in more detail in the next Chapter. It so erratic that Lorenz dispaired of predicting the weather by simulation of this dynamical model. The chaotic attractor, translated back into the original context of air currents in the atmosphere, provides a model for *atmospheric turbulence.*

**The actual microstructure of this object, which we call *Lorenz's mask,* is described further in the next chapter, and still further in *Part Three* of this Series.**

## 3.4.  ROSSLER'S BAND

Inspired by Lorenz's discovery, and aided by an analog computer with stereo 3D display, Rössler set out to find the simplest dynamical systems with chaotic attractors. Among others, he discovered the simple folded band described in this section. Later, Crutchfield (1980) found the same phenomenon in the Duffing model for the forced pendulum.

**3.4.1.**   Here is an electronic analog of Duffing's forced pendulum. In the black box, upper right, is an electronic analog of a damped pendulum. The meters read the instantaneous current through, and voltage across, the load resistor on top of the box. The forcing oscillation is generated by the isolated oscillator, center, which also sends a strobe pulse to the storage scope, left. A dot written on this screen will persist.

This is much like R. Shaw's experimental setup for the Birkhoff bagel, in the forced Van der Pol device described in Section 3.2.

**3.4.2.** Recall, from *Part One,* these mechanical devices used by Lord Rayleigh to model the violin string (later studied by Duffing) and the clarinet reed (later studied by Van der Pol). Without being forced, the oscillation of one dies away, while the other's is self-sustained. When forced, both will oscillate.

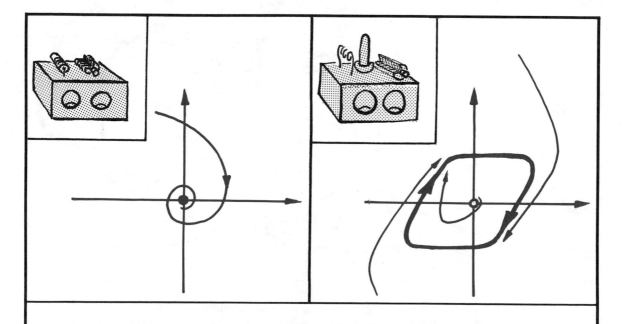

**3.4.3.** In the context of electronic analog devices, we have these two devices: without forcing, one wants to be still, the other to oscillate, as shown in these phase portraits. When forced, both will oscillate, as described in *Part One, Periodic Behavior.*

**From these two devices, extensively described in *Part One: Periodic Behavior,* much of dynamics has evolved. We return now to the electronic analog of the Duffing device.**

REVIEW: With the forcing oscillator set close to the natural frequency of the damped electronic pendulum, there are *two periodic attractors* in the ring model for the three-dimensional state space of the combined system *(Part One,* Panel 4.3.8). Thus, our strobed storage scope will show a dotted curve asymptotically approaching a point. There are two such attractive points in the strobe plane. *Which attractor* our strobed (dotted) trajectory ends up at depends on *which basin* the initial point is in. (The initial point may be chosen by the experimentalist before turning the device on.) The two basins are separated (in the three-dimensional ring model) by a scrolled surface, the inset of a periodic saddle (panel 4.3.13 in *Part One).* In the strobe plane, they are separated by a teardrop-shaped curve (panel 4.3.12 in *Part One).*

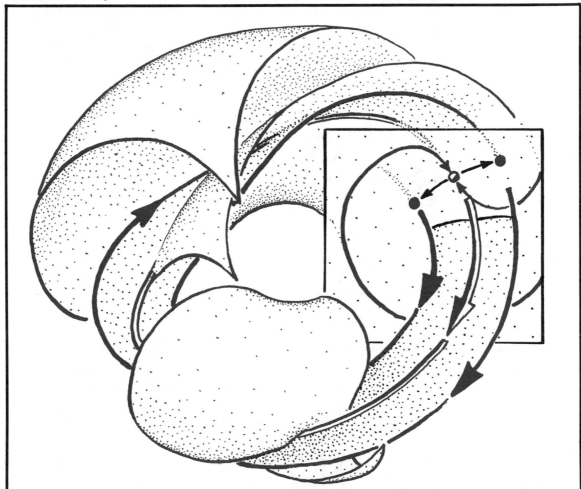

**3.4.4.** Here is the *separatrix* of the isochronous oscillations of the electronic Duffing device. As the *inset* of a periodic saddle, it is not a limit set, but it is *repelling.* In the strobe plane, it appears as a *teardrop-shaped curve.* Meanwhile, the *outset* of the periodic saddle, although not a limit set either, is *attractive.* It is a *twisted band* (shaded black in this drawing) bounded by the two periodic attractors. This outset band meets the strobe plane in a short curve segment, shown here in heavy black. Just as the inset (separatrix, red) is repelling, the outset band (black) is attracting.

**Now let's watch this attractive outset band, as we increase the frequency of the driving oscillator.**

**3.4.5.** For a while, as the driving frequency increases, we find an increasing number of periodic attractors. These are the *harmonics,* described in some detail in *Part One,* Chapter 4 (for example, panel 4.4.17). In the strobe plane observed by the storage scope, they appear as a growing set of isolated points.

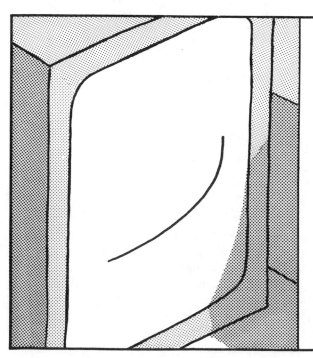

**3.4.6.** But after we increase the forcing frequency sufficiently, this entire arc appears as an attractor. It is the strobed view of the attractive outset band of the periodic saddle. The attracted trajectory hits it repeatedly, randomly walking throughout its length.

**3.4.7.** If we leave the *frequency* fixed but change the *phase* of the strobe pulse, we find the arc rotates, flexes, stretches, and folds.

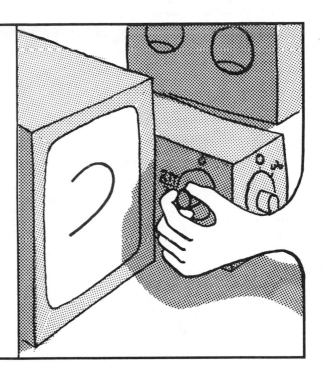

**3.4.8.** Putting these strobe views together around the ring model, we obtain a three-dimensional picture of this unusual attractor, first observed by Rössler in another dynamical system.

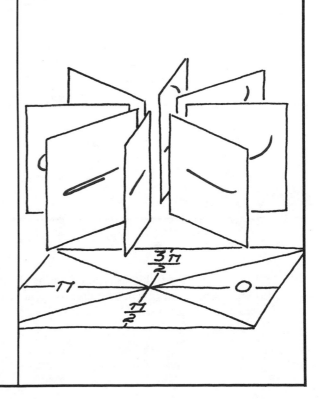

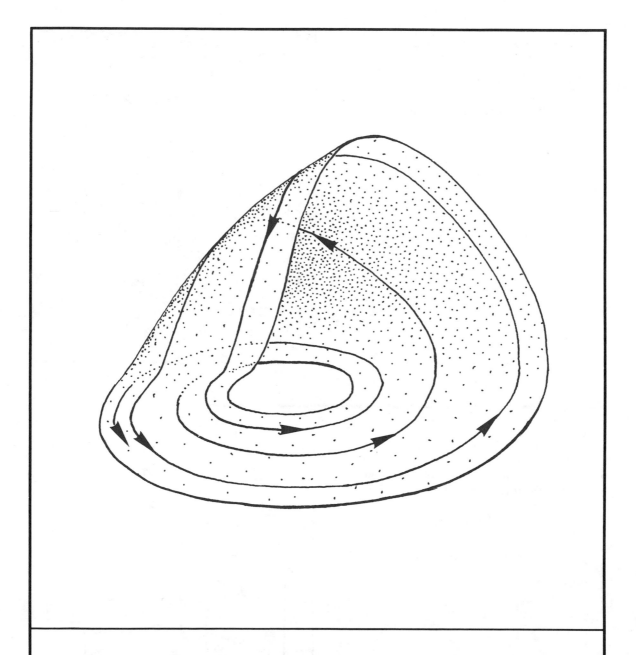

**3.4.9.** Here is the full Rössler band, in the Duffing system. Like the Birkhoff bagel and the Lorenz mask, it appears to be a slightly thickened surface. A more detailed picture of its rich microstructure is presented in the next Chapter. Keep in mind, meanwhile, that these attractors are not static objects. They determine the dynamic behavior of an attracted trajectory.

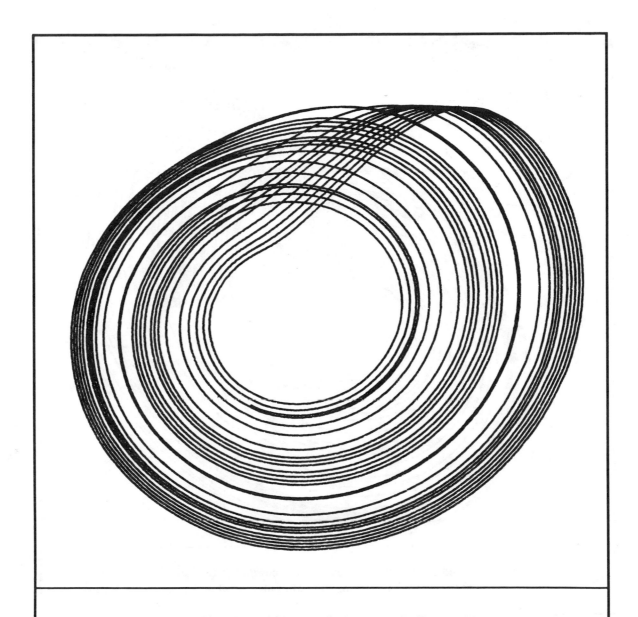

**3.4.10.**   Here is the full Rössler band, as seen by Rössler in his original system. (See the Appendix for the equations, this computer drawing courtesy of R. Shaw.) This view is straight down from the top, so the height of the fold (shown in the preceding panel) is fore-shortened. The trajectories do not actually cross in 3D.

There are many other unusual attractors waiting to be discovered by pioneers with analog and digital computers. This is one of the last frontiers of the *local theory* of dynamical systems.

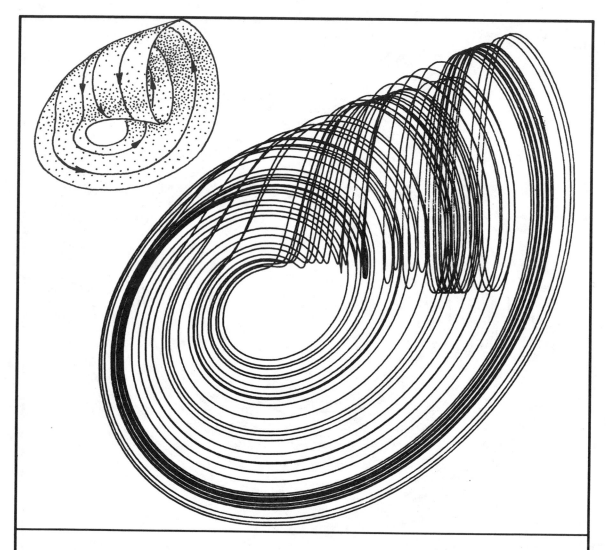

**3.4.11.**   Here is a related experimental object, also discovered by Rössler, which we call the *funnel.* (See the Appendix for the equations, this computer drawing courtesy of R. Shaw.)

The trajectories attracted to these attractories asymptotically approach almost every location in the thickened surface. Of course, the motion of such a trajectory is precisely determined by the mathematical model. Yet because the smallest uncertainty in the determination of the actual position of the trajectory at a given moment implies an enormous uncertainty later on, the future of the trajectory along the attractor is *apparently chaotic.* Hence, these experimental objects are called *chaotic attractors.* They may not be either attractors or chaotic in any rigorous mathematical sense, however. All this will be clarified in the next Chapter.

# 4.   Attributes of Chaos

There are many reasons for calling the unusual limit sets, found experimentally and described in the preceding chapter, *chaotic*. In this chapter we will describe some of these reasons, which have received considerable attention in the literature.

## 4.1.  UNPREDICTABILITY

Although the large-scale attractors are aspects of a dynamical system which are fully deterministic in the formal mathematical sense, the behavior of an trajectory attracted to such an attractor is totally unpredictable, in the long run. This is the reason these extended limit sets have earned the name *chaotic attractors*. In this section we explain this paradox, originally emphasized by Lorenz (1962, 1963).

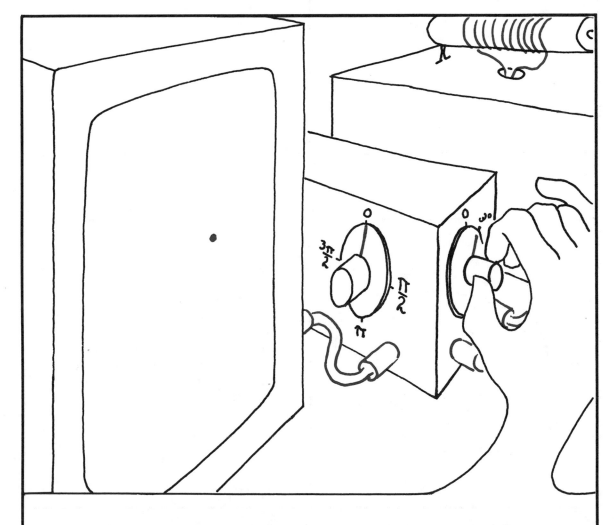

**4.1.1.**   In the preceding section, we observed this situation, in the electronic Duffing device, before the appearance of Rössler's band. The attracted trajectory returns repeatedly, at exact intervals, to the same point in the strobe plane. This is the epitome of *predictable* behavior.

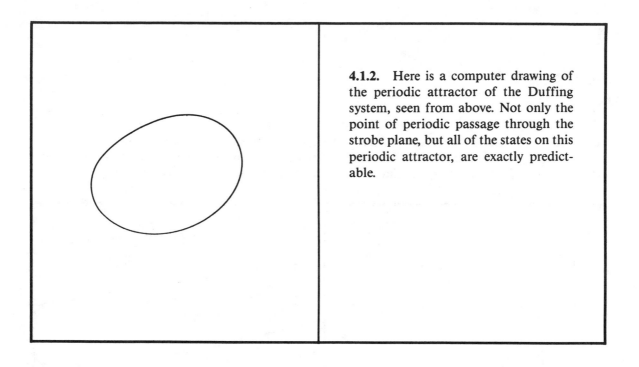

**4.1.2.** Here is a computer drawing of the periodic attractor of the Duffing system, seen from above. Not only the point of periodic passage through the strobe plane, but all of the states on this periodic attractor, are exactly predictable.

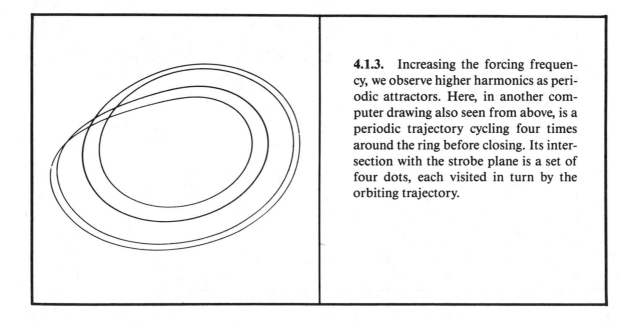

**4.1.3.** Increasing the forcing frequency, we observe higher harmonics as periodic attractors. Here, in another computer drawing also seen from above, is a periodic trajectory cycling four times around the ring before closing. Its intersection with the strobe plane is a set of four dots, each visited in turn by the orbiting trajectory.

**This motion is completely predictable. After observing a few cycles, we can predict, based on one strike of the strobe plane, exactly where the next few will strike.**

**4.1.4.** Increasing the forcing frequency further, we obtain an extended attractor. Also seen from above in this computer drawing, there are several bands within a figure like Rössler's band. The intersection with the strobe plane is a set of thick arcs. (The thickness is explained in Section 4.4.) Although the orbiting trajectory passes through these thick arcs periodically, we are unable to make long range predictions based on one strike.

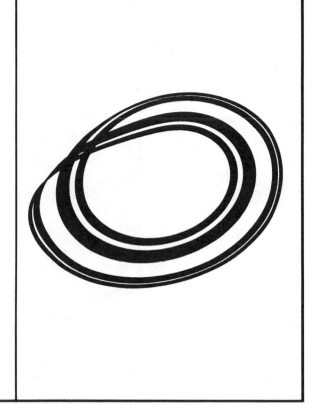

**Although the motion is fully deterministic in the mathematical sense, it is rather unpredictable in the experimental sense. This is one reason this motion is called *chaotic*.**

The successive passages of the trajectory, orbiting the Rössler-like band, are experimentally rather unpredictable, because (1) we do not know the exact position of the trajectory at a given moment, (2) a small difference in this current position leads to an enormous difference in position later on, and (3) the trajectory will eventually come arbitrarily close to any point on the thick bands.

Property (2), characteristic of all chaotic limit sets, is called *sensitive dependence on initial conditions*. Property (3), also characteristic of chaotic limit sets, is called *topological transitivity*. Related to the *ergodic hypothesis* of statistical physics, this just means that a single trajectory pierces every little region in the limit set. These conditions are described further in the next section.

**We now explain why these three conditions lead to unpredictability.**

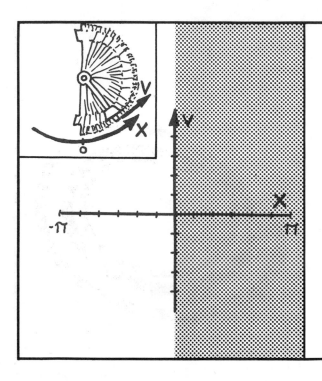

**4.1.5.** The *precision of our measurement* of the pendulum's state (displacement and velocity), at a given time, may be regarded as an *amount of information.* Here, for example, suppose we know only that the state is in the shaded half of the state space. Our information, then, is only that the pendulum is to the right of bottom. We know nothing of the speed of its motion, not even its direction. This is a *small amount of information* about the instantaneous state of the system.

**The more precise the measurement, the smaller is the region known to be occupied by the state of the system, and the more information we have about it.**

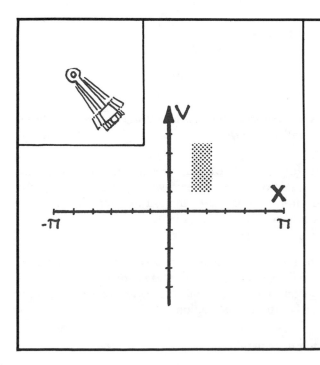

**4.1.6.** In this case, our measurement is more precise. The state is known to be in the small shaded box. Thus the displacement and velocity are known, within small intervals of error. We have a *considerable amount of information* about the the state of the pendulum.

**4.1.7.** Carried to extremes, if our measurement were infinitely accurate, the region of uncertainty would be a point, and our information would be infinite. This is the assumption in the *mathematical context.*

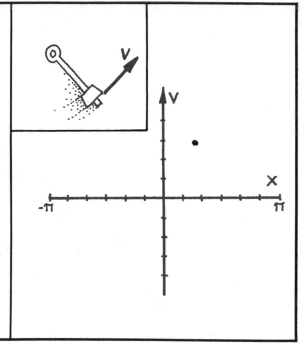

**4.1.8.** But in the *experimental context,* there is always a *region of uncertainty,* due to the realities of observational instruments, recording media, and the Uncertainty Principle. Here, we see this region by enlarging the preceding drawing.

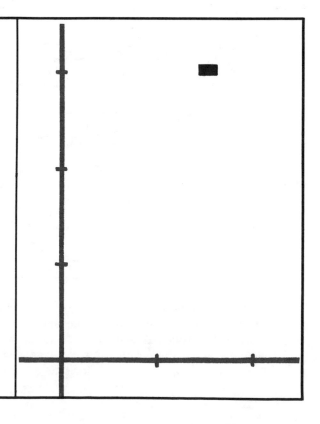

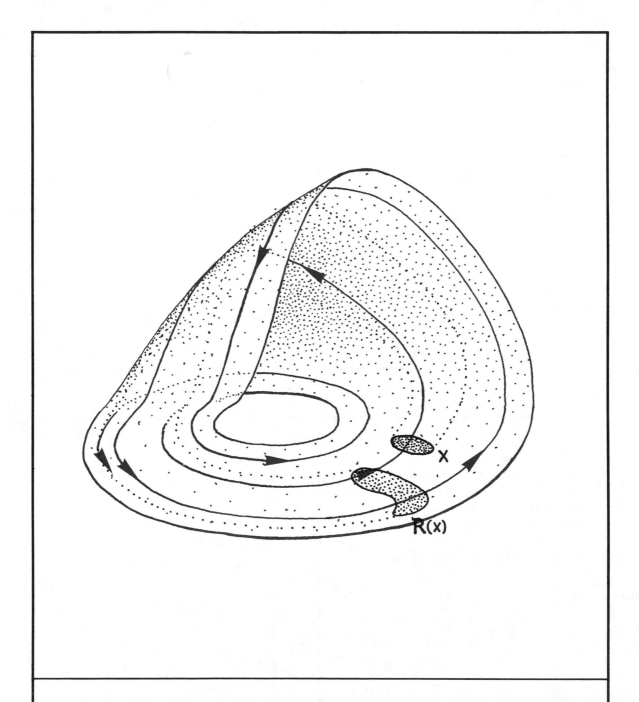

**4.1.9.**  Returning to Rössler's band, let us begin with a region of uncertainty, shown in black here and labeled x, within the strobe plane. After approximately one cycle, this track passes through the strobe plane again in the set shown here in black, labeled R(x). But the track *expands*. So the original region, x, has expanded to the larger set R(x). After this expansion, *we have less information* about the state of the system.

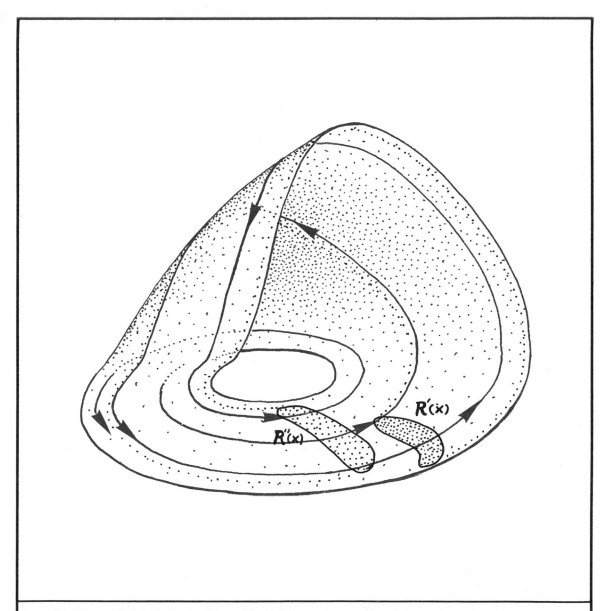

**4.1.10.**   We relabel R(x) by R′(x). The track continues to expand. And after another similar period of time, it has passed through the strobe plane again, in the black set R″(x). The original region, x, its first return, R′(x), and its second return R″(x), comprise the beginning of an infinite sequence of sets. These are getting wider and wider. And so *we have less and less information* about the state of the system, as time goes on.

**In fact, no matter how small the initial region, the successive strikes of its trajectories through the strobe plane will spread in this way. The cause of this spreading is explained in the next section.**

So this, at last, is the meaning of *unpredictability* in the context of chaotic attractors. *Any small error* in the measurement of the current state (inevitable) eventually *leads to total ignorance* of the position of the trajectory, within the chaotic attractor.

## 4.2.  DIVERGENCE AND INFORMATION GAIN

The basic dynamical feature of chaotic attractors is *bounded expansion,* or *divergence and folding* together of trajectories within a bounded space. This feature implies *sensitive dependence on initial condition,* originally emphasized by David Ruelle, and *gain of experimental information,* introduced by Robert Shaw. In this section we explain these implications. The connection between divergence and characteristic exponents (CEs) is given in the following section.

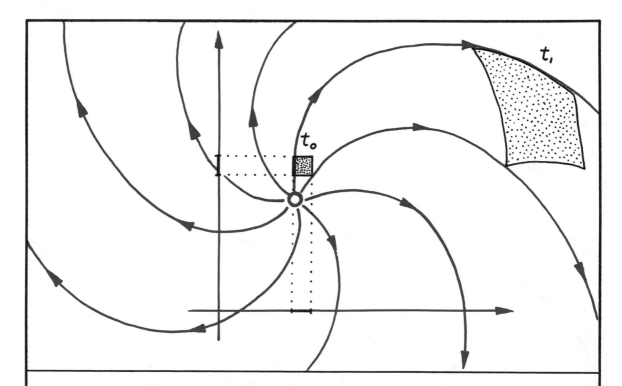

**4.2.1.**   Suppose we have a dynamical system with a planar state space, and a repelling point. After a careful measurement of both variables at time $t_0$, we have determined that the state of the system is in a *small region near the point repellor.* The track of this region, along trajectories of the dynamical system, spirals away from the repellor, *expanding as it goes.* Thus, at a later time, $t_1$, the track of the initial region is a larger region, as shown here. Supposing that *we do not remeasure* the state of the system at this later time. Then the information we originally had, together with our knowledge of the phase portrait of this system, add up to the knowledge that the system is in a state in the larger region, nothing more. But the larger uncertainty means we have *less information at the later time* than we had at the time of the initial measurement. The *divergence of the trajectories* leaving a repellor *implies loss of the information* obtained from an initial measurement.

On the other hand, the divergence of trajectories leaving a repellor, together with new measurements at a later time, implies a *gain of information*. Now let's carefully follow this divergence, and its attendant information gain, in four steps:

* measure the initial state of the system,
* watch this region expand, while initial information is lost,
* remeasure the state of the system, increasing current information,
* extrapolate backwards, gaining information on the initial state.

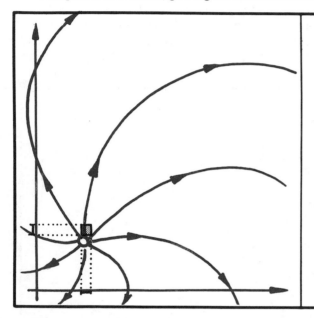

**4.2.2.** At the initial time, we *measure the state of the system as accurately as possible,* within the limitations of the given laboratory instruments. The position of the initial point in the state space is thus a small region, such as this rectangle. Its sides are the experimental errors in the values of the separate coordinates, such as position and velocity of the pendulum.

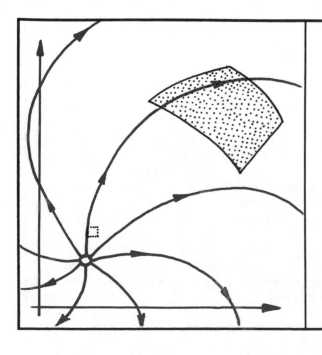

**4.2.3.** After an interval of time, the initial region flows outwards from the repelling point, along the diverging trajectories of the dynamical system, as we see here. The initial region grows into this *larger region.* Information about the current state seems to be decreasing, as we know less and less about the actual state of the system as time goes on.

**4.2.4.** But at this later time, we *re-measure* the state of the system, again with the best accuracy of the laboratory apparatus. Now we have increased our information about the system at the later time.

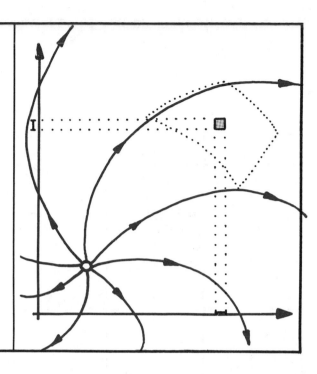

**4.2.5.** Finally, we flow the larger region *backwards* in time to its original position, as a small rectangle. and along with it, we flow the small rectangle it contains. This becomes the immeasurably small dot within the initial rectangle, as shown here. As this is smaller than the initial rectangle, we have *more information* about the initial state, because of the second set of measurements, than we could possibly have known at the beginning.

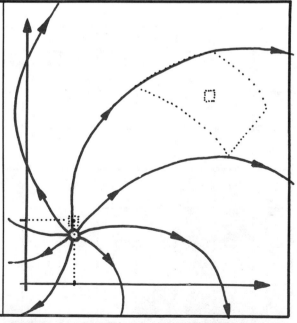

By this sequence — measure, flow, remeasure, reflow backwards — we have obtained *more information* about the state of the system at the initial time than we did with the initial measurement (with the same instruments).

**To emphasize the actual gain of information provided by diverging flow, let's repeat this sequence with the state space coarse-grained by cells indicating the limit of precision of the measuring and recording apparatus.**

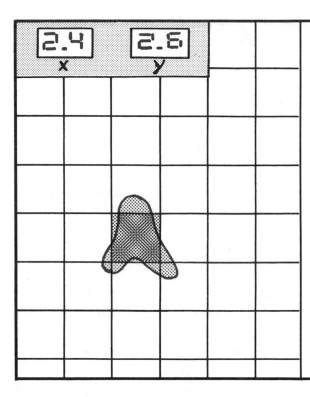

**4.2.6.** In this armchair experiment, we suppose that the measuring apparatus is digital, with data bins 0.1 units wide. Thus, all values of x between 2.35 and 2.45 are thrown into the 2.4 bin by the measuring and recording process, and likewise for values of y. Here we see the state space, coarse-grained by these bins. The red shading represents a region known mathematically to be occupied by the initial state of the dynamical system. But the black shaded bin represents the region known experimentally, according to the most accurate measurement possible, with the assumed instruments, at the initial time. The system, with almost 100 percent certainty, occupies the cell labeled (2.4,2.6) by the measuring instruments, as shown in the corner box.

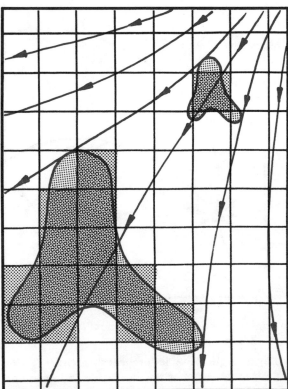

**4.2.7.** After a period of diverging flow, the initial red cell has expanded so as to cover many experimentally distinguishable cells. Without a new measurement, we have *less information now about the current state* than we initially had about the initial state. We do not know which of the thirteen black shaded bins the system now occupies. However, if we now make a new measurement and extrapolate backwards in time, we will have *more information now about the initial state* than we did originally. Acknowledging our capacity to make measurements any time we wish, we see that *diverging flow provides increasing information about initial states. Information is gained* in diverging flows.

**4.2.8.** Conversely, near a point attractor, the flow is convergent. An initial region shrinks smaller and smaller. Here, initial points, known through measurement to be distinct, eventually become experimentally indistinguishable. Extrapolation backwards of current measurements may tell us nothing about the initial state of the system. Thus, *convergent flow provides decreasing information about initial states. Information is lost* in converging flows.

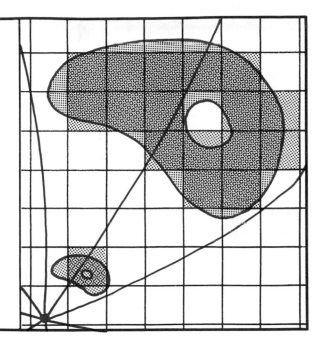

We have illustrated the concepts of *information gain and loss, or flow,* in flows near repelling and attracting points. Similar concepts apply to repelling and attracting limit cycles, and, as we shall see in the next section, to chaotic attractors. We turn now to the related concept of *sensitive dependence on initial conditions.*

**4.2.9.** Suppose we have two adjacent initial conditions, near a repelling point. Because of the divergence of trajectories in this flow, the trajectories from these two initial points diverge. After some time, the two initial states have flowed to final states which are far apart. Thus, in this context, a *small change in initial state results in a large change in final state,* after a short time of evolution of the system. This, called *sensitive dependence on initial conditions,* is a characteristic feature of chaotic attractors. These, like the repelling point illustrated here, have diverging trajectories, as we shall see in the next section.

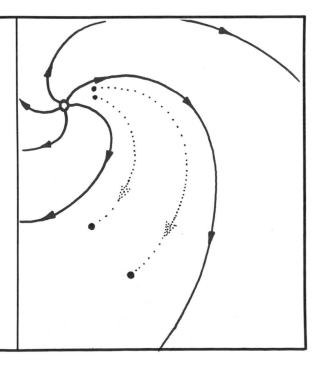

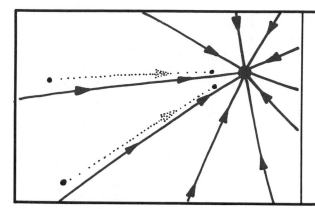

**4.2.10.** Conversely, in the converging flow near an attracting point, a large change in initial state results in a smaller change in final state, after a short time. We may call this *insensitive dependence* on initial conditions.

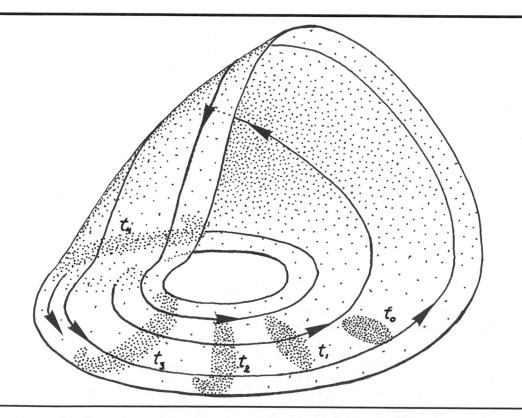

**4.2.11.** Finally, suppose that a set, such as the Rössler band pictured here, is almost completely filled by a single solenoidal trajectory. Then a small region of initial states at the initial time, $t_0$, moves along to a more extended region at a later time, $t_1$. After a long while, this set must be pulled and twisted so as to cover most of the entire band. For the solenoidal trajectory pierces the initial region infinitely often, and these initial points flow along the solenoid and almost fill the band. This situation, called *topological transitivity,* is not implied by diverging trajectories alone, but is nevertheless an observed feature of all experimentally-known attractors. This may be due to the constraints of reality, causing experimental dynamicists to study a single trajectory.

## 4.3.  EXPANSION, COMPRESSION AND CHARACTERISTIC EXPONENTS

Divergence (or equivalently, information gain, or sensitive dependence) plus transitivity imply un-predictability, as described in Section 4.1. In this section, we show how divergence and convergence, or expansion and compression, occur simultaneously near chaotic attractors.

**How can compression to the attractor, and expansion along the attractor, happen simultaneously? Here we explain the geometry of this paradox, in the case of Rössler's band.**

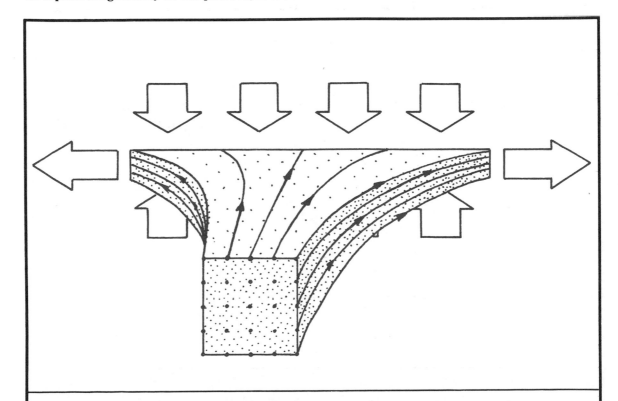

**4.3.1.**   Consider a flow in three dimensions, like the flow near a periodic saddle, which is attractive in one direction, and repellent in another. For *periodic saddles,* this is described by two characteristic multipliers: one CM inside the unit circle, the other outside. (See Section 2.3.) Alternatively, we describe the saddle behavior with two characteristic exponents: one CE to the left of the imaginary axis, and one to the right. (See Section 2.6.) For our present purpose, we prefer CEs. But these CEs may be calculated for trajectories which are not closed, as long as they are *recurrent* like the transitive solenoidal trajectory in the Rössler band, illustrated in Section 3.4.

**In this flow, horizontal information is gained, while vertical information is lost. The negative CE describes the rate of vertical convergence, while the positive CE describes the rate of horizontal divergence.**

All the chaotic attractors illustrated in the preceding chapter are *thick surfaces* in three dimensional space. (The source of this thickness, an infinite number of surfaces compacted close together, is explained in the next section.) A transitive trajectory in each is saddle-like, as in the preceding panel. But the *attracting direction is perpendicular* to the thick surfaces, which are therefore attractive. Meanwhile, the *repelling direction is tangent* to the thick surfaces, so the flows along these attractors are *diverging*.

**At the same time, trajectories *converge* towards the attractor, and *diverge* along it, saddle-like. Here is the way the Rössler attractor manages endless divergence within a bounded region, in five steps.**

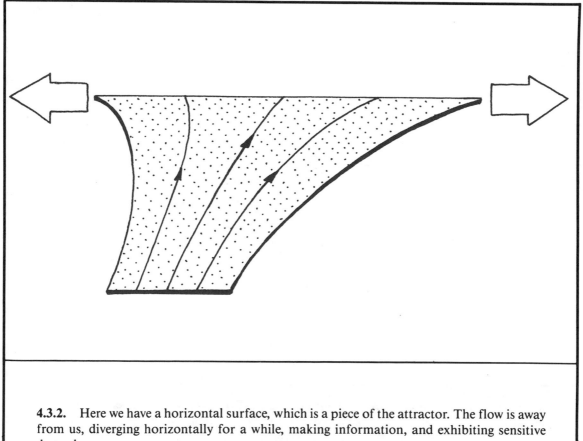

**4.3.2.** Here we have a horizontal surface, which is a piece of the attractor. The flow is away from us, diverging horizontally for a while, making information, and exhibiting sensitive dependence.

As the flow progresses, this piece of surface grows at the far end. We will track this growth.

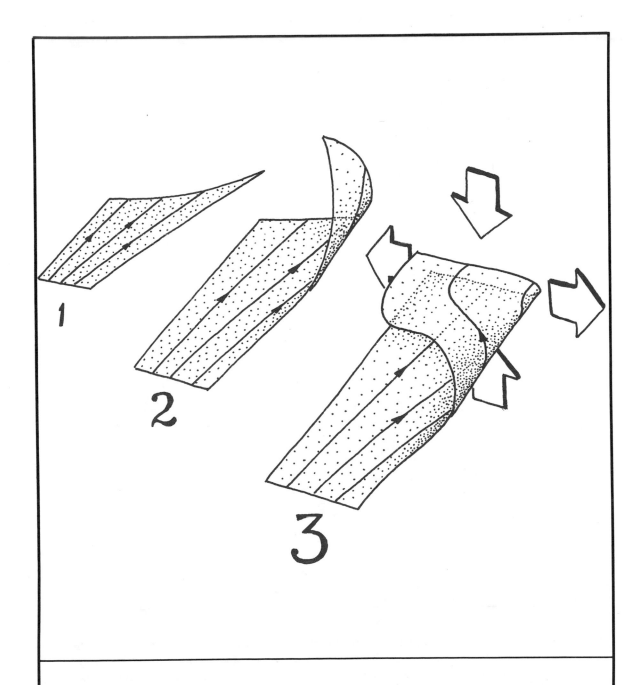

**4.3.3.** In step 1, the back extends away from us, and widens as it goes, because of divergence. The right wing is rising. Step 2, the back extends and widens further, but the widening is all to the right and upwards. The growing right wing is folded up and to the left. Step 3, the back extends further, widens more to the right, and the right wing is folded further upwards and to the left, until it is parallel to the unchanged orientation of the left wing.

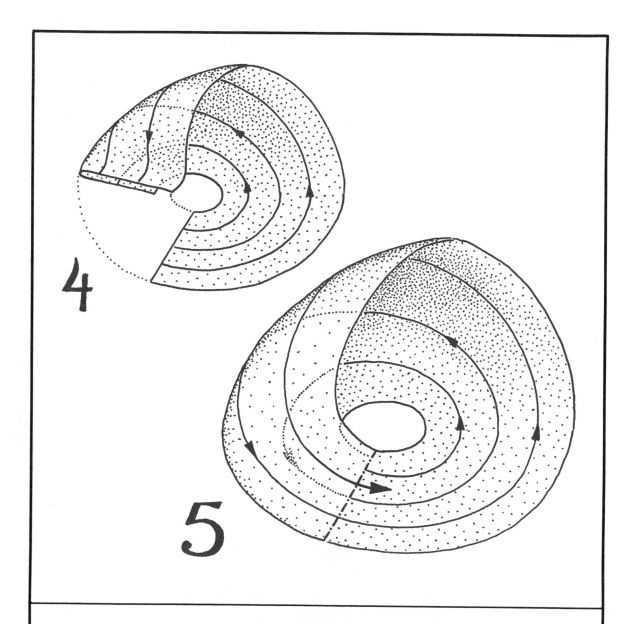

**4.3.4.** In step four, the process is continued, and we find that the rearward growth of the surface is actually along a circle, bringing it eventually back and around to meet the front. Step five, it closes. In fact, it does not exactly close as a surface. What we have described is a *thick surface,* composed of infinitely many layers, like flaky pastry, filo, or croissant dough. This is explained in some detail in the next section.

**Try following two trajectories around the band, and you will see that they endlessly diverge in a bounded space, as transitive solenoids. They keep on diverging from each other in the short term, while never succeeding in getting too far from each other, in the long run.**

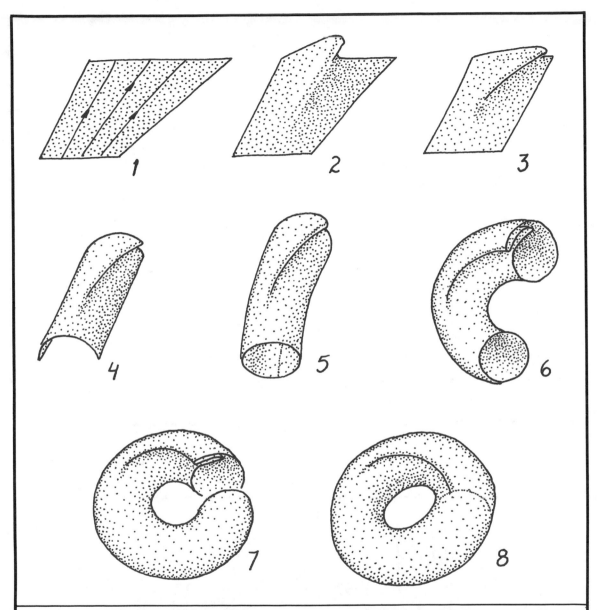

**4.3.5.** Birkhoff's bagel also expands endlessly in a bounded space, as shown in this eight step model. In step 1, we start with a diverging flow on a piece of surface, as before. Step 2, the back grows away from us, and a fold begins to form in the middle. In step 3, the back extends further away from us, and the fold is pressed down flat, like a pleat. This drawing has been shrunk a bit to save space. Step 4, the back grows further and the fold is pressed flatter. Taking more of the sides into view, we see they bend downwards. The drawing is shrunk again, to fit in the panel. In step 5, more of the object comes into view, and we see that the sides join at the bottom like a pleated cylinder. Step 6, following the growth at the back of the cylinder, we see it is bending around a circle. In step 7, the bent pleated cylinder is joining itself, to make a torus. Finally, it closes, as a thick surface.

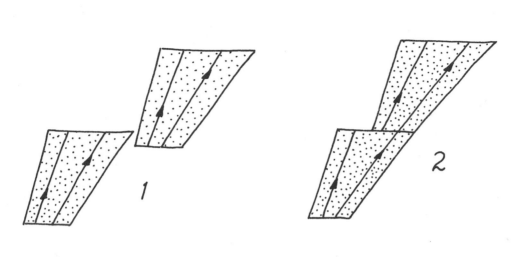

**4.3.6.** Lorenz's mask is also endlessly expanding in a bounded space. We will describe this in seven steps. First, take two copies of our usual piece of surface, with a diverging flow on each. Join them, as shown in step 2.

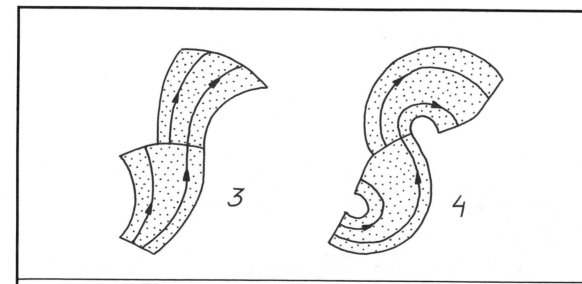

**4.3.7.** In step 3, taking more of the flow into view, we see the surfaces bending. In step 4, the flow of the back edge away from us begins to curve all the way around. Likewise, the flow into the front edge is seen to come from around a bend, also.

**To get ready for the next step, rotate the S-shaped model (step 4) clockwise a half turn.**

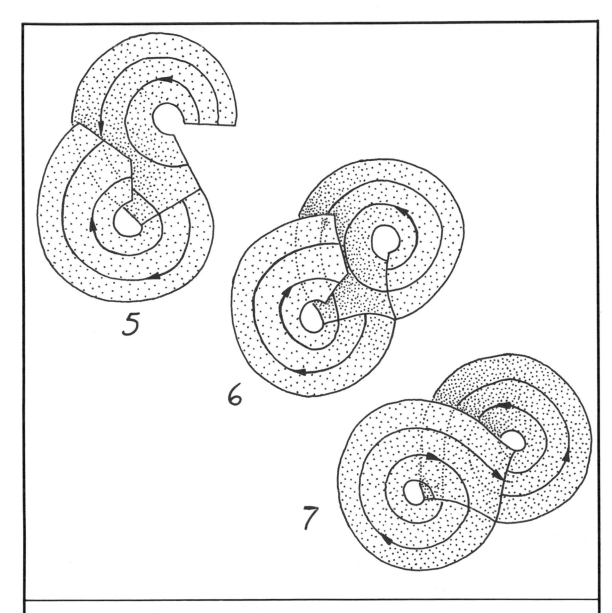

**4.3.8.** In these last three steps, the front and back edges are extended further along the flow, bending further until they join. These joints are as thick surfaces, as we shall see in more detail in the next section.

These objects have a fractal dimension, somewhere between two and three. They also have CEs, like a periodic saddle.

To complete our models for these three chaotic attractors, we zoom in on the fractal microstructure of thick surfaces, in the next section.

## 4.4.   FRACTAL MICROSTRUCTURE

The folding required to expand endlessly in a bounded region requires an infinite microstructure. Here we explain this feature of chaotic attractors, again using Rössler's band for illustration.

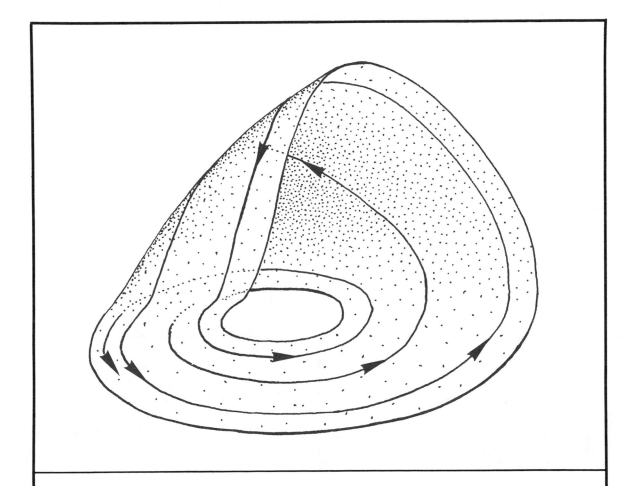

**4.4.1.**   Here is the Rössler band, as the folded thick surface constructed in the preceding section, in five steps. As distinct trajectories of a dynamical system may never join, this object cannot possibly be a simple surface, with two layers glued together.

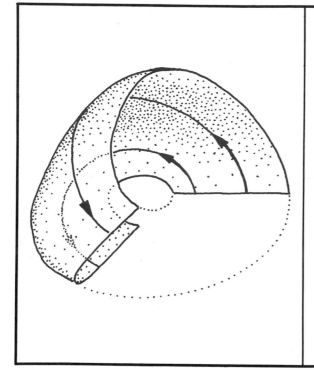

**4.4.2.** Let's follow the progress, as time marches on, of a *Poincar*é section of the thick surface. This appears to be a line-segment at first. As we shall soon see, it is actually a *thick line-segment*. First it extends backwards away from us, curving to the left and around a circle. At the same time, it widens and folds over. Eventually it reaches double its original width, folding all the way over, and comes back to the Poincaré section as a U-shaped channel.

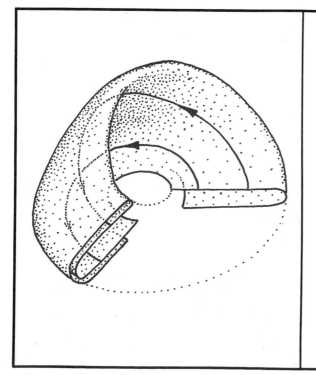

**4.4.3.** Now we understand that the cross-section of the band is not an interval. It must be a folded interval with two layers. Let's follow the evolution of this folded interval as it goes around, repeating exactly the steps above. Starting another turn as a U-shaped channel, the stretch and fold produces a double-U-shape on return to the Poincaré section.

**4.4.4.** Now we know that the section is not a line-segment, and it's not a U-channel either. Starting a third turn as a double-U, the folding action of the band creates a quadruple-U on next return to the Poincaré section. And so on!

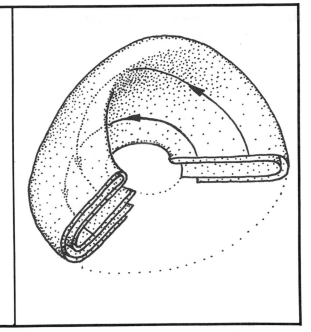

**4.4.5.** After countless repetitions, the original interval of section as expanded, folded, and returned in countless layers. These accumulate in a certain pattern. To examine this pattern, we cut again in a cross-section. This one, which we call the *Lorenz section,* cuts through the Poincaré section.

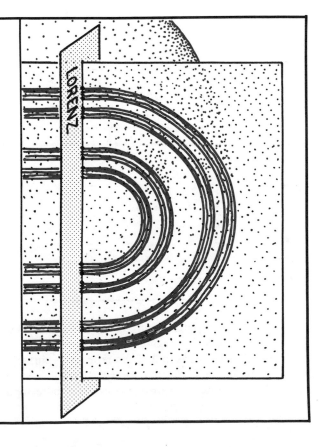

**4.4.6.** Turning the Lorenz section face front, we see a single dot corresponding to each layer of the filo dough of Rössler's band. The number of dots is infinite. But, they have a pattern. There are gaps within gaps within gaps.

**4.4.7.** The pattern may be reconstructed in a sequence of steps called *Cantor's process*. First take a line segment, at 1. Then remove a smaller segment from somewhere within, making a gap, as in 2. Then repeat this surgery on each of the two remaining segments, obtaining 3, and continue forever. If at each step you take away the middle third of a segment, this is the *middle thirds process*. But there are many other possibilities.

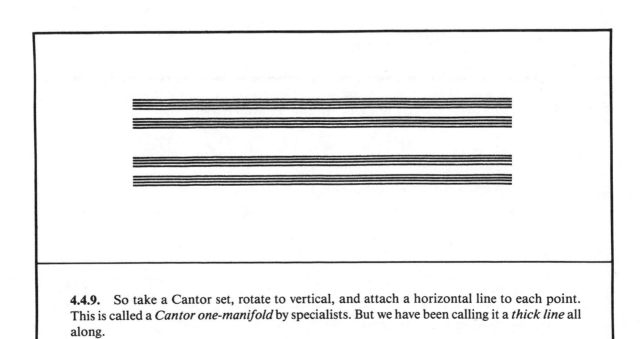

**4.4.8.** For example, this construction removes two intervals in each surgery. It is the *middle fifths process*. We cannot pin down exactly which process is needed to reconstruct the Lorenz section of the Rössler band. But it is definitely this kind of thing, called in general a *Cantor set*.

**4.4.9.** So take a Cantor set, rotate to vertical, and attach a horizontal line to each point. This is called a *Cantor one-manifold* by specialists. But we have been calling it a *thick line* all along.

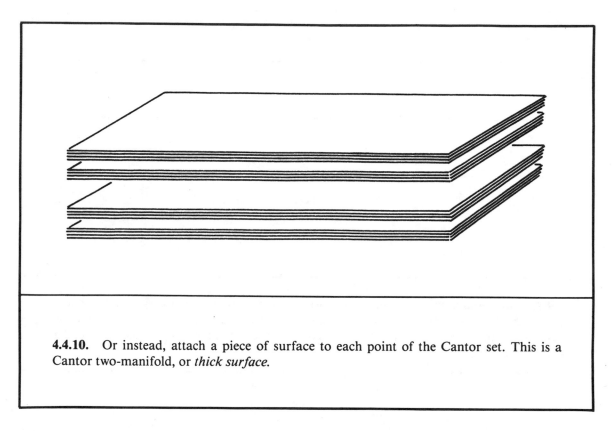

**4.4.10.** Or instead, attach a piece of surface to each point of the Cantor set. This is a Cantor two-manifold, or *thick surface*.

By *fractal microstructure,* we just mean a thick line or surface, more-or-less. We also must allow creases, folds, and so on. For more information on fractals, and their fractal dimensions, see the excellent books by Mandelbrot and Stewart, listed in the Bibliography.

**All the experimentally known chaotic attractors are characterized by this kind of fractal microstructure, as well as by the divergence of trajectories, measured by characteristic exponents. Relationships between the fractal dimension and the characteristic exponents are a current research topic.**

## 4.5.   NOISY POWER SPECTRA

The normal impulse of an experimentalist, upon sighting a complex time series, is to take its power spectrum. As we have seen in Section 2.7, the power spectrum from a periodic attractor is a discrete, or line, spectrum. This technique has been very successful with the chaotic attractors. But the power spectra of chaotic attractors are continuous, or *noisy*.

**4.5.1.**   The power spectrum of a time series is computed by an arduous algorithm. The longer the time series input, the more accurate the power spectrum output. The spectrum contains about half enough information to recreate the original time series. It records the frequencies and powers, but not the phases, which are used in the reconstruction, as shown in Section 2.7.

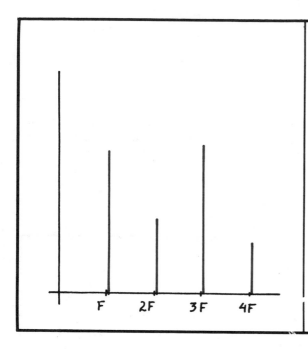

**4.5.2.** This is the power spectrum of a typical periodic attractor. Each line, over an integral multiple (octave) of the fundamental frequency of the oscillator, indicates by its height the power contributed to the oscillatory motion in that octave. This is called a *discrete spectrum.*

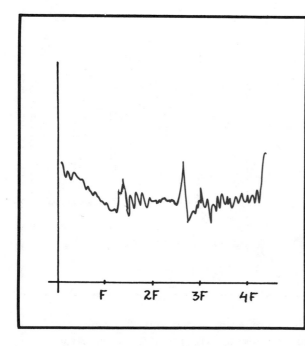

**4.5.3.** This, in contrast, is the power spectrum of a typical chaotic attractor. There is activity at every frequency. This is called a *continuous spectrum.*

With experience, we might be able to recognize attractors from the power spectra of the time series produced by one coordinate of the state space, if we had enough examples on file. This is like the fingerprint strategy for criminal identification.

**4.5.4.** This periodic attractor in three dimensions is fully described by three time series, one for each coordinate. The power spectrum of one of these is shown here.

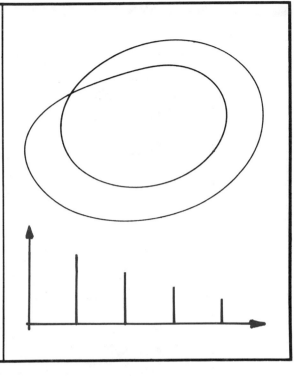

**4.5.5.** This chaotic attractor in three dimensions is also fully described by three time series, the coordinates of a transitive solenoidal trajectory. The power spectrum of one of these might look like this: a discrete spectrum with a little noise added.

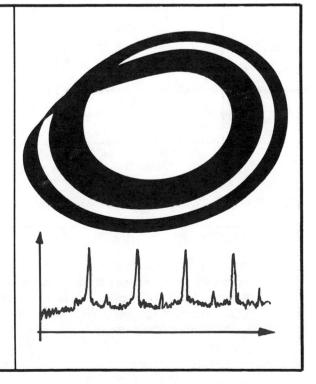

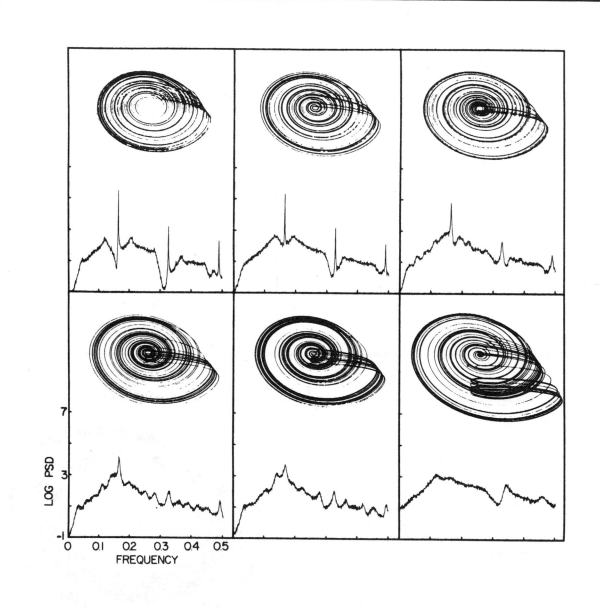

**4.5.6.** These chaotic attractors (Rössler bands and funnels) are increasingly chaotic, as shown by the increasing levels of the noise (continuous spectra) in their power spectra, shown below in each case. This is actual data from analog simulations (Crutchfield et al, 1980). Note that the spikes, indicating approximately periodic behavior, are lost in the noise in the lower right example.

| NAME | PORTRAIT | TIME SERIES | SPECTRUM |
|------|----------|-------------|----------|
| point | | | |
| closed orbit | | | |
| Birkhof Bagel | | | |
| Lorenz Mask | | | |
| Rössler Band | | | |
| Rössler Funnel | | | |

**4.5.7.** Here is a summary table of the exemplary attractors we have presented, with sketches of their characteristic output. One could wish for an extension of this table, showing all possible attractors likely to arise in experiments and applications. But at this point, that's a big wish.

## 4.6.  CONCLUSION

This completes our visual introduction to the *local behavior* of dynamical systems, begun in *Part One*. By local behavior, we mean the behavior of trajectories on or near a *single attractor*. It is important to keep in mind that a typical dynamical system has *many attractors* and basins. In applications, the location of these may be more important than the particular local behavior of each attractor (point, cycle or chaos). We repeat here, in ending this part of our story, that *the identification of experimental attractors with limit sets of mathematical models is not yet fully justified in dynamical theory.*

**In the next volume, *Part Three, Global Behavior,* we will turn to the *global behavior* of dynamical systems.**

# Appendix: Systems of Equations

*Example: 2d.*
*Section: 3.4.*
*Type: Forced spring.*
*Origin: Duffing, 1908.*
*Space: Ring, $R^2xS^1$.*
*Coords: displacement, x.*
   *velocity, y.*
   *driving phase, θ*
*System:*

$$x' = y$$
$$y' = (-1/m) \{a_3x^3 + a_1x + cy\} + Fcos\theta$$
$$\theta' = \omega$$

*Remarks: mass, m*
    *restoring force of spring, $a_1x + a_3x^3$, $a_1 > 0$,*
    *hard spring, $a_3 > 0$*
    *linear spring, $a_3 = 0$*
    *soft spring, $a_3 < 0$*
    *coupling strength, F*
    *driving frequency, ω*

*Example: 4b.*
*Section: 3.2.*
*Type: Forced, self-sustained oscillation.*
*Origin: Rayleigh 1888 (see Volume 1)*
*Space: Ring, $R^2xS^1$.*
*Coords: current, x.*
   *voltage, y.*
   *driving phase, ω*
*System:*

$$x' = y$$
$$y' = (-1/CL) \{x + By^3 - Ay\} + Fcos\theta$$
$$\theta' = \omega$$

*Remarks: capacitance, $C > 0$*
    *inductance, $L > 0$*
    *characteristic function of vacuum tube, $Bv^3 - Av$, $A,B > 0$*
    *coupling strength, F*
    *driving frequency, ω.*

*Example: 4c.*
*Section: 3.2.*
*Origin: Van der Pol, 1922.*
*System :*

$$x' = y$$
$$y' = (-1/CL) \{x + (3Bx^2 - A)y\} + F\cos\theta$$
$$\theta' = \omega$$

*Remarks:  version of 4b, obtained by differentiation.*

*Example: 4d.*
*Origin : R. Shaw, 1980.*
*Section: 3.2.*
*System:*

$$x' = y + F\cos\theta$$
$$y' = (-1/CL) \{x + (3Bx^2 - A)y\}$$
$$\theta = \omega$$

*Remarks:  version of 4c, obtained by moving the force to the first equation.*

*Example: 5.*
*Section: 3.3.*
*Type: Polynomial.*
*Origin: Lorenz, 1962.*
*Space: Euclidean, $R^3$.*
*Coords: x, y, z.*
*System :*

$$x' = 10(y\text{-}x)$$
$$y' = x(28\text{-}z)\text{-}y$$
$$z' = xy\text{-}(8/3)z$$

*Example: 6.*
*Section: 3.4.*
*Type: Polynomial.*
*Origin: Rössler, 1968.*
*Space: Euclidean, $R^3$.*
*Coords: x, y, z.*
*System:*

$$x' = -(y+z)$$
$$y' = x + y/5$$
$$z' = 1/5 + z(x\text{-}5.7)$$

# Bibliography

Abraham, Ralph H., 1983, *Is there chaos without noise?* In: Chaos Days at Guelph, P. Fischer and W. R. Smith, eds., Dekker, New York.

Crutchfield, R. J. Donnelly, J., D. Farmer, G. Jones, N. Packard, and R. Shaw, 1980, *Power spectra analysis of a dynamical system,* Phys. Lett. 76A: 1-4.

Guckenheimer, J. and P. Holmes, 1983, *Nonlinear Oscillations, Dynamical Systems, and Bifurcations of Vector Fields;* Springer-Verlag, New York.

Lichtenberg, A. J., and M. A. Lieberman, 1982, *Regular and Stochastic Motion;* Springer-Verlag, New York.

Helleman, Robert H. G., (ed.), 1980, *Nonlinear Dynamics, (Annals, vol. 357);* New York Academy of Sciences, New York.

Hilton, Peter, (ed.), 1976, *Structural Stability, the Theory of Catastrophes, and Applications in Sciences, (Lecture Notes in Math., v. 525);* Springer-Verlag, New York.

Mandelbrot, B., 1982, *Fractals;* Freeman, San Francisco.

Ruelle, D., 1980, *Strange Attractors;* La Recherche: 108.

Shaw, R. S., 1981, *Strange Attractors, Chaotic Behavior, and Information Flow;* Z. Naturforsch., 36a: 80.

Sparrow, C., 1982, *The Lorenz Equations;* Springer-Verlag, New York.

Stewart, I., 1982, *Les Fractals;* Belin, Paris.

*Announcing the*
*Visual Mathematics*
*Library*

## — Film Series —

**VISMATH LIBRARY FILM SERIES**

## The Lorenz System

### by Bruce Stewart

The first in a series of high resolution computer animated movies on nonlinear dynamics, *The Lorenz System* shows a visual example of elementary chaos. Edward Lorenz's model of thermally driven convection is explained in a standard 16mm color film of 25 minutes duration. Because the subject itself is three-dimensional and dynamic, the film format can bring fundamental ideas from the research frontier within the reach of non-specialists.

The film introduces the fluid dynamical model leading to the dynamical system, and constructs phase portraits of the system for a wide range of parameter values. Ideas are introduced step by step, beginning with the notion of phase space itself. The presentation is entirely visual, without equations, but with frequent captions explaining the important ideas. The major bifurcations in the Lorenz system are seen, and the mainifold outstructure emanating from the equilibria is examined in the laminar, pre-chaotic, and chaotic regimes. The geomoetry of period doubling cascades is observed.

*The Lorenz System* is suitable for college-level students of differential equations, fluid mechanics, or nonlinear oscillations. Anyone who deals with nonlinear models of dynamics (in physics, chemistry, biology, ecology) can gain valuable insight from this film.          *25 minutes, color, 16mm.*

**VISMATH LIBRARY FILM SERIES**

## Chaotic Chemistry

### by Robert Shaw, Jean-Claude Roux
### and Harry Swinney

Experimental data from a stirred chemical reactor, plotted according to the graphical scheme of nonlinear dynamics, reveals a geometric figure essentially identical to the famous Rössler attractor of chaotic dynamics. (Section 3.4 of *Part Two, Dynamics: The Geometry of Behavior*). This film shows the experiment, the graphical scheme, and the structure of the reactor, in exquisite detail, using state-of-the-art computer graphics equipment. A brief written description accompanies the movie.
*20 minutes, black & white, 16mm*

**VISMATH LIBRARY FILM SERIES**

## Chaotic Attractors of
## Driven Oscillators

### by J.P. Crutchfield

This movie studies a series of classic nonlinear oscillators. The technique used is that of animated Poincaré sections. This is the temporal animation of cross sections through an attractor. A single Poincaré section is made by collecting the oscillator's position and velocity at a fixed phase of the driving force. The animation then plays back in time successive sections as the driving phase advances. The technique allows one to easily see and study the folding and stretching geometry around the attractors.

The movie presents five chaotic attractors taken from three different nonlinear oscillators. The first three examples come from Shaw's variant of the driven Van der Pol osciallator. (See Sec. 3.2 of *Part Two, Dynamics: The Geometry of Behavior*). The first exhibits the folding action of three "ears" on a torus attractor. The second "ribbon" attractor is the consequence of a period-doubling route to chaos. The final Van der Pol example reveals a complex attractor with visible fractal leaves. The movie illustrates the first attractor's symmetries by superimposing sections.

The fourth attractor comes from Duffing's oscillator (See Chapter 4, *Part One, Dynamics: The Geometry of Behavior*). With its thick fractal structure, it is reminiscent of oriental brush-stroked characters. The final example is the driven damped pendulum. As this attractor is spatially periodic and of infinite extent, a "five-well" segment is shown. With the animation it appears as a train of ocean waves continually breaking on a beach.

The movie *Chaotic Attractors of Driven Oscillators* was filmed during the fall of 1981 and premiered at Dynamics Day La Jolla, 4-6 January, La Jolla, California. A brief written description accompanies the movie.
*12 minutes, black & white, 16mm*

## To Order

Please see enclosed Price List and complete the order form attached. Advance pay't required.

*Introducing:*

# The Science Frontier Express Series

## VOLUME ONE
### SCIENCE FRONTIER EXPRESS SERIES

## The Dripping Faucet as a Model Chaotic System

### by Robert Shaw

One of the most exciting recent developments in dynamical system theory has been the emergence of a better understanding of the **"chaotic transition,"** the change of behavior of many systems from periodic to nonperiodic behaviour. In this work, the author shows that the pattern of drops from a simple faucet makes such a transition, as the tap is slowly opened. This physical example is used to address the important general question: if a system is chaotic, how chaotic is it?

Information theory, the author argues, provides the appropriate tools for sorting out mixtures of determinism and chaos. Although this work describes the very latest results in the application of information theory to dynamical systems, the presentation is as nontechnical as possible. The text is illustrated by more than 60 pictures, and every effort has been made to make the material accessible to a wide audience. The result is a remarkably clear discussion of the concepts of "entropy" and "information" in the context of dynamical systems — easily readable, for example, by students of Shannon's book on information theory. The book ends on a more philosophical note, with a personal view of the issues which will loom largest in the future development of the subject. *111 pages, 63 illustrations*

## VOLUME TWO
### SCIENCE FRONTIER EXPRESS SERIES

## On Morphodynamics
### by Ralph Abraham

*On Morphodynamics* includes selected papers written by Dr. Ralph Abraham on models for pattern formation processes, morphogenesis, and self-organizing systems, showing the evolution of the **complex dynamical systems** concept over a fifteen year period. The works indicate a range of applications spanning the physical, biological, psychological, and social sciences. *225 pp., 55 pp illustrations*

The volume includes:
1. *Stability of models, 50 pp, 1967.*
2. *Introduction to morphology, 126 pp, 1972.*
3. *Psychotronic vibrations, 4 pp., 1973.*
4. *Vibrations and the realization of form, 18 pp., 1976.*
5. *The macroscopy of resonance, 8 pp., 1976.*
6. *Simulation of cascades by videofeedback, 5 pp., 1976.*
7. *The function of mathematics in the evolution of the noosphere, 15 pp., 1980.*
8. *Dynamics and self-organization, 28 pp., 1980.*
9. *Dynamical models for thought, 22 pp., 1981.*

## VOLUME THREE
### SCIENCE FRONTIER EXPRESS SERIES

## Complex Dynamical Systems
### by Ralph H. Abraham

*Complex Dynamical Systems* includes selected recent papers on complex models for physiological systems. *125 pp., 43 pp. illustrations*

The volume includes:
1. *Categories of dynamical models, 25 pp., 1983.*
2. *Dynamical models for physiology, 6 pp., 1983.*
3. *Complex dynamical systems, 5 pp., 1984.*
4. *Chaos and intermittency in an endocrine system model (with H. Koçak and W.R. Smith), 41 pp., 1981.*
5. *Orbital plots of dynamical processes, (with A. Garfinkel), 19 pp., 1983.*
6. *Cortisim (with A. Garfinkel), 11 pp, 1983.*
7. *Endosim, a progress report, 9 pp., 1984.*

(Eff. 10/84)

## Order Form/Price List for:

**AERIAL PRESS, INC.**
P.O. Box 1360 - Santa Cruz, CA 95061
(408) 425-8619

### Dynamics: The Geometry of Behavior

| | Price | Ship/Handling |
|---|---|---|
| **PART THREE: GLOBAL BEHAVIOR** | $ 26.00 | $ 2.00* |

Pre-publication discount: orders placed before 12/31/84 receive 10% discount on price shown.

| | Price | |
|---|---|---|
| Part One: Periodic Behavior | 32.00 | 2.00* |
| Part Two: Chaotic Behavior | 26.00 | 2.00* |
| Disk Two: Chaotic Attractors in 3D | 20.00 | 2.00* |
| Disk One: Periodic Attractors in the Plane | 20.00 | 2.00* |

*Prices are for shipping inside the U.S. only. For shipments outside the U.S., shipping costs are: Canada & Mexico: $4.00 for each item ordered. South America: $8.00 for each item ordered. Japan: order from Yurinsha, Ltd., Hongo, P.O. Box 63, Tokyo, 113-91, Japan. All other countries: Order from Birkhauser, Elisabethenstrasse 19, CH-4010, Basel, Switzerland.

### SCIENCE FRONTIER EXPRESS SERIES

| | Price | Ship/Handling |
|---|---|---|
| Volume One: The Dripping Faucet as a model | $ 15.00 | $ 2.00** |
| Chaotic System by Robert Shaw | | |
| Volume Two: On Morphodynamics, Selected Papers by Ralph H. Abraham | 25.00 | 2.00** |
| Volume Three: Complex Dynamical Systems, Selected Papers by Ralph H. Abraham | 15.00 | 2.00** |

**Prices are for shipping inside the U.S. only. For shipments outside the U.S., shipping costs are: Canada & Mexico: $4.00 for each item ordered. South America: $8.00 for each item ordered. All other countries: $12.00 for each item ordered.

### VISUAL MATHEMATICS LIBRARY FILM SERIES

| | Price | Ship/Handling |
|---|---|---|
| The Lorenz System by Bruce Stewart | $190.00 | $5.00*** |
| Chaotic Chemistry by Robert Shaw, Jean-Claude Roux and Harry Swinney | 190.00 | 5.00*** |
| Chaotic Attractors of Driven Oscillators by J. P. Crutchfield | 190.00 | 5.00*** |

***Prices are for shipping inside the U.S. only. For shipments outside the U.S., shipping costs are: Canada & Mexico: $8.00 for each item ordered. South America: $12.00 for each item ordered. All other countries: $16.00 for each item ordered.

**PAYMENT MUST ACCOMPANY ORDER. PLEASE INCLUDE SHIPPING CHARGES.**

---

## Aerial Press, Inc.

P.O. Box 1360    Santa Cruz, CA 95060    (408) 425-8619

Name _____

Street _____

City, State, Zip _____

To charge to your VISA or MasterCard, please complete the following:

Card # _____   Exp. Date: _____

Signature _____   Phone #: _____

| Item(s) Ordered | Price | Sh/Handl | Quantity | Total |
|---|---|---|---|---|
| 1. | | | | |
| 2. | | | | |
| 3. | | | | |
| 4. | | | | |
| 5. | | | | |
| 6. | | | | |
| 7. | | | | |
| 8. | | | | |

California Residents add 6% sales tax

**Payment Must Accompany Order.**   (U.S. Dollars) TOTAL

Payment must be in U.S. Dollars. For orders outside the U.S., please send payment via either an International Money Order, or a check with American Banking Association (ABA) computer numbers, drawn on a U.S. bank.